when MORNING
COMES

Wallace D. Chappell

when MORNING COMES

ABINGDON PRESS

Nashville New York

WHEN MORNING COMES

Copyright © 1966 by Abingdon Press

Library of Congress Catalog Card Number: 66-19806

SET UP, PRINTED, AND BOUND BY THE
PARTHENON PRESS, AT NASHVILLE,
TENNESSEE, UNITED STATES OF AMERICA

To DR. and MRS.
CLOVIS G. CHAPPELL

*who have salted my life
and lighted my world . . .
with tender memories
and sincere affection*

PREFACE

The church's supreme need for a negative day is a positive faith.

The first sermon in this series deals with the tidings that Philip the evangelist shared with the Ethiopian eunuch—"he preached unto him Jesus." It is where he began. It is where we begin and then approach other meaningful certainties found in the New Testament.

We have the firm belief that the great texts of Scripture are the shining, optimistic, hopeful ones. We do not need preaching that is filled with night. We need to hear sermons proclaimed that tell us the morning has come. It is hoped that the themes discussed here will guide us to assurance in our convictions and joy in our witness.

CONTENTS

VICTORIOUS ENCOUNTER 11

Then the Spirit said unto Philip, Go near, and join thyself to this chariot. (Acts 8:29)

STRESSING THE SIGNIFICANT 20

Jesus came into Galilee, preaching the gospel of the kingdom of God, and saying, The time is fulfilled, and the kingdom of God is at hand: repent ye, and believe the gospel. (Mark 1:14-15)

A VALIANT FAITH 29

For I am not ashamed of the gospel of Christ: for it is the power of God unto salvation to every one that believeth; to the Jew first, and also to the Greek. (Rom. 1:16)

THREE CHEERS 39

I have told you this so that you can share my joy, and that your happiness may be complete. (John 15:11 Phillips)

THE POWER OF PRAISE 48

At midnight Paul and Silas prayed, and sang praises unto God. (Acts 16:25)

DIVINE PROMISES 57

Every promise of God finds its affirmative in him [Christ]. (II Cor. 1:20 Phillips)

THAT RADIANT PLEA 65

Welcome one another, then, as Christ has welcomed yourselves, for the glory of God. (Rom. 15:7 Moffatt)

• BUILDING CHRIST'S CHURCH 74

Thou art Peter, and upon this rock I will build my church. (Matt. 16:18)

DRAWN TO THE CROSS 81

I, if I be lifted up from the earth, will draw all men unto me. (John 12:32)

WHEN MORNING COMES 89

When the Sabbath was over, just as the first day of the week was dawning . . . an angel of the Lord came down from Heaven, and rolled back the stone. (Matt. 28:1-2 Phillips)

AFTER PENTECOST 97

When the day of Pentecost was fully come, they were all with one accord in one place. (Acts 2:1)

And they continued steadfastly. (Acts 2:42)

THE YEARNING CHRIST 105

I stand knocking at the door. If anyone listens to my voice and opens the door, I will come into his house and dine with him, and he with me. (Rev. 3:20 Phillips)

VICTORIOUS ENCOUNTER

*Then the Spirit said unto Philip, Go
near, and join thyself to this chariot. (Acts
8:29.)*

Conversion is not primarily understanding a belief but
sharing a relationship.

Here on the desert road between Jerusalem and Gaza
is the scene of a victorious encounter, one of many that we
find in the New Testament. A prominent personage, the
treasurer of a North African state, meets personally the
living Lord and, in the spell of this radiant fellowship,
returns to his homeland with gladness.

Yet, as always, the eunuch's conversion experience was
dependent upon an intermediary—one whom the Spirit
had compelled to be his envoy. In this particular instance
that messenger was Philip the evangelist.

Let us then look at this victorious encounter in the light
of three facts: the mission of Philip, the tidings he declared, and the results that were achieved.

I

The Ethiopian treasurer was returning to his native
land after celebrating Pentecost at Jerusalem. However, it

is evident that he had not found that which he had traveled so far to find. That he was an earnest seeker and later a joyful receiver the scripture leaves no doubt. But it was his need that had not been met and his thirst that had not been quenched which caused the Holy Spirit to give Philip his task: "Go up and join this chariot."

Is not the Christian religion basically a missionary movement—a summons to serve? "Go and make disciples"; "Feed my sheep"; "You shall be my witnesses"; "Go up and join this chariot."

One of the startling facts of this story is that the Spirit directed Philip to approach one man with the good news. When next we hear of Philip he is preaching at Azotus, which had been one of the chief cities of the Philistines. From there he preached in various towns until he arrived in Caesarea, the major city of Palestine. But here in the text he is declaring the gospel to a single individual.

Thus the Holy Spirit was doing in the days of the young church what our Lord was always stressing in his own ministry. There was a demoniac who needed soundness of mind. There was a teacher who needed birth from above. There was a prostitute by a well who needed someone to guide her out of the shadows. There was a thief on a cross who needed the redemptive touch in the hour of death. He never neglected the one for the crowd—the man for the mass. He himself was the shepherd who could not be satisfied with almost all. How much our statistic-minded church of today needs to look away from a fold nearly full to a lamb sadly lost!

So the commission of Philip embodies these two features: the Spirit's command and the preacher's obedience. "Rise and go"—"he rose and went." I wonder if I would have been willing. The evangelist had just finished conducting an amazing crusade in Samaria. Luke declares that multitudes gave heed to what he said and that as a result of such an awakening the whole city rejoiced. (Acts 8:6, 8.) Now he goes to a desert road to speak to a single foreigner.

This may be far more difficult than addressing a throng. Are we willing to assume a task that may be unspectacular yet essential for Jesus' sake?

Dwight L. Moody preached to a hundred million people but he never allowed himself to forget the need of personal contact. He said, "I made it a rule that I would not let a day pass without speaking to someone about their soul's salvation, and if they did not hear the gospel from the lips of others, there would be three hundred sixty-five in a year that would hear the gospel from my lips."

This, then, was the mission of Philip: to approach one man and present to him the glad tidings of the faith.

II

What were the tidings that the evangelist presented to the eunuch? Luke says simply, "Philip preached unto him Jesus." (Acts 8:35.) Now we would wish to know the full content of Philip's sermon. Unfortunately we do not have it. However, since he preached Jesus to the treasurer, it is highly probable that he preached the vital things about Jesus to him.

Without doing an injustice to the scriptures, let us suggest three cardinal points that most likely were given emphasis.

I think that, in the first place, Philip preached to the eunuch *the Jesus of Galilee*. We are aware that the scripture the eunuch was reading was from what is now the fifty-third chapter of Isaiah. This, of course, deals with the suffering servant. Whether the prophet was anticipating the Christ or had in mind some local general or his entire nation is not really relevant. Jesus so fulfilled the function of this sacrificial office that he became the answer to the prophecy.

It is, however, not presuming upon the scripture, I contend, to say that Philip probably presented Christ alive before he spoke of his atoning death. He must have witnessed to the incarnate Lord.

Here we can only imagine what the evangelist reported. It is perfectly logical and in line with New Testament thought to suggest, however, that if Philip spoke of the incarnation it was in terms of a "God-man" who had come to redeem.

This is the heart and soul of the gospel. And we must not shrink from either word—God or man.

Our Lord was a man. He was a man who could feel emotion. "O Jerusalem, Jerusalem, which killest the prophets, and stonest them that are sent unto thee; how often would I have gathered thy children together, as a hen doth gather her brood under her wings and ye would not." (Luke 13:34.)

He was a man who could express genuine anguish. Read again his words in Gethsemane: "My soul is exceeding sorrowful, even unto death" (Matt. 26:38).

He was a man who could know physical want: "I thirst," he said from the cross (John 19:28).

But it was not simply man that made blind people see. It was not simply man that made deaf people hear and lame people walk.

It was more than man that stood at the cave-tomb of a dear friend and said, "Lazarus, come forth" (John 11:43).

It was more than man who walked from his grave alive forevermore saying to his disciples, "Ye shall be witnesses unto me unto the uttermost part of the earth" (Acts 1:8).

He was a man; he was the human Jesus of Galilee. He was more; he was the eternal Christ of God.

Philip preached to the eunuch *the Jesus of Calvary*. Here we do not have to lean upon our imagination to surmise. Scriptural evidence affirms this point.

Luke says, regarding what we have already referred to (Isa. 53:7), "Philip opened his mouth, and began at the same scripture, and preached unto him Jesus." (Acts 8:35.) And the good news for these first disciples was the Crucifixion and Resurrection. It should be for us.

Probably while in Jerusalem the eunuch had heard

15

about Jesus and his death. But the report came from hostile lips and no doubt our Lord was spoken of in derision and scorn. Now he was hearing the gospel in its truth and simplicity. One need not read far in Luke's Acts to see that the disciples never wandered too far from the Cross in their preaching.

Some days ago an elderly gentleman visited our church. He lives in a community several miles away, and after the service I volunteered to drive him home. Not being too familiar with the residential neighborhood where he lives, I inquired as to some spot familiar to both of us. "Do you know where Calvary Methodist Church on the Hillsboro Road is?" I asked. "Yes," he replied. "I do not live far from Calvary." And neither did Philip. Further, one may guess that as we read, "[He] went on his way rejoicing," the eunuch, too, had come to have this experience as his abiding place.

Then, I think that Philip preached to the eunuch *the Jesus of Easter*. The Ethiopian could scarcely have rejoiced because of a slaughtered sheep or a dumb lamb or a taken life.

Those followers of our Lord proclaimed always the death of their Savior. But they never stopped there. They spoke of the cross and the empty tomb in the same breath.

Philip would not have quit at Calvary. By itself that would have been bad news. Luke says he told the eunuch good news. But if Philip did not stop with a grave neither would this earnest seeker have desired baptism unto a deceased leader, no matter how great he had been. Men are looking for life.

I don't know but that the saddest words Jesus ever said are these spoken to the Jews: "Ye will not come to me, that ye might have life" (John 5:40).

We quibble over unpardonable sins. I think there is but one: to be offered life and not to take it.

The eunuch rejoiced because new life had come to him. This was possible because of the eternally living Christ. Listen to the Master's own words: "Because I live, ye shall live, also" (John 14:19). "I am alive. You will be alive." What courageous cheer that glorious news should bring!

III

We look finally at the consequence of this encounter. Here is the radiant conclusion: "He [the eunuch] went on his way rejoicing" (Acts 8:39). What a thrilling ending! What a victorious encounter!

If there is anything our modern world, perhaps even our present church, is short on it is not gloom. And if there is anything our current religious society is long on it is most certainly not gladness.

It is not our intention here that you think we are speaking in the context of amused entertainment. The eunuch's cause for rejoicing went far deeper than mere emotional pleasure. His mood was that of the soul set to music. The very joy of Jesus had become part of his life in this act of *receiving* the Savior.

This is not simply the philosophy of the young church about which we read in Acts. It is the very lifeblood of the gospel. Notice, for instance, how the Gospel of Luke begins: "The angel said unto them [the shepherds], 'I bring you good tidings of great joy'" (Luke 2:10). And the Gospel of Luke ends with the disciples returning to Jerusalem from Bethany "with great joy" (Luke 24:2). That is, the beginning and the conclusion of the Gospel is joy.

We know very little about the man from Ethiopia up to this point. Was he a Jew? We do not know. Had he been exposed to the Jewish scripture? Perhaps; we are not certain. Had he heard of Christ before? Most likely, but again there is no evidence.

It is apparent that he was going back to his homeland with frustration instead of fulfillment. His had been a pilgrimage without peace—a journey without joy. But on the road to Gaza he encountered Philip and, more important, Philip's Lord, and for the eunuch that desert region began to blossom as the rose.

There is one other point. If the Ethiopian treasurer found happiness in receiving the Savior, there would be the continued gladness of *revealing* the Savior. We do not have a later account of this man but we do know the record of many New Testament converts. Hence, we are not reading something into the story that is not found in all Christian history.

"He went on his way rejoicing." It is altogether possible that it was through this man that the gospel arrived in

Northeastern Africa. Did we speak of an ending? This victorious encounter was just the beginning. "He went on his way rejoicing." This, then, was the joy of not only what he had felt but of what he could share, for Christianity has not only the happiness of experience but of expression.

That noted saint John Duncan of Scotland was once walking along a street in Edinburgh. On his face was the glow of a joyful discovery. "Dr. Duncan," remarked a passerby, "you look as if you had heard good news." "The best news," he answered; "Jesus saves."

Thus receiving led to revealing. I am sure this was the experience of the man from Ethiopia. I am sure it will be your experience if you give your life to Christ!

STRESSING THE SIGNIFICANT

Jesus came into Galilee, preaching the
gospel of the kingdom of God, and saying,
The time is fulfilled, and the kingdom of God
is at hand: repent ye, and believe the gospel.
(Mark 1:14-15.)

The ministry has drawn considerable fire from its critics
for failing in this century to proclaim the essential. Ministers, teachers, trained laymen alike have all been criticized
for not declaring what their judges have called primary.

"Fighting the devil where he used to be," one faultfinder
exclaims. "Preachers are answering questions nobody is
asking," charges another. "They aim at nothing and hit
it," protests a third.

Now granted that many of these adverse critics are much
too outspoken and severe, still there is some truth in their
caustic accusations. We, as the church's spokesmen, all
too often have magnified the trivial and minimized the
tremendous. In truth, we deserve the condemnation of
Ezekiel: "Who unto the foolish prophets" (Ezek. 13:3).

It would seem to me, therefore, that it would be wise for
us to look to the master Preacher as to what should be
foremost in our proclamation. Mark says that Jesus entered
Galilee with four imperatives in his heart and on his lips.

I

"The time is fulfilled." What time? The time of the advent of the kingdom. This is the hour ordained of God. This is the hour foreseen by prophets. The Saviour has arrived. The Deliverer has appeared. "Joy to the world! the Lord is come."

The night watchman of the colonies used to walk the streets crying, "Eleven o'clock . . . twelve o'clock . . . one o'clock," and so on through the night. Mark says that Jesus came preaching and his first sermon was, "It is kingdom-time."

How glorious was this news when first it was declared across the hills of Galilee. Those who had stumbled attempting to keep the law now rejoiced, for love had made its entrance.

One can almost picture old Simeon in the temple. How long he had anticipated the coming of the dawn! When he saw the child Jesus he took him in his arms and gave praise to God. I love his words as Dr. Moffatt translates them:

> Now, Master, thou canst let thy servant go,
>   and go in peace, as thou didst promise;
> for mine eyes have seen thy saving power,
>   which thou hast prepared for all peoples,
> to be a light of revelation for the Gentiles,
>   and a glory to thy people Israel. (Luke 2:29-32.)

How glorious, I say, was this news when it was first proclaimed.

21

But it should not have lost one bit of its radiance for our day. This thrilling proclamation is always relevant. It is timely and it is timeless. "The time has come." The day is always today for the coming of Christ into the hearts of men. The time is always now for the high business of the soul to be transacted.

A dear friend told me how he sought one day to win a cultivated woman for Christ. He indicated that she knew little of what it meant to be a follower of the faith. Finally he asked, "Did you know that God has set a definite date for your salvation?" She replied that she did not know. "He has," my friend said. "If I show you that he has, will you keep the engagement?" When she replied in the affirmative, he said to her, "Now is the accepted time; behold, now is the day of salvation" (II Cor. 6:2). The time is always now. That hour is always present. The day is always today. It is kingdom-time.

II

"The kingdom of God is at hand." Jesus spoke more about this subject than any other. We find more than 140 references to the "Kingdom" in the Gospels. What did the Master mean by this dynamic announcement, "The kingdom has arrived"?

Its meaning carries with it, in the first place, a very personal implication. The kingdom had arrived because the king had arrived. One never enters the kingdom until the king enters him. Jesus said, "Fear not, little flock, for it is your Father's good pleasure to give *you* the kingdom." But he also said, *"I* am come that they [men] might have life" (John 10:10). We will say in a moment that the "kingdom of God" means the rule of God in the world. But its first meaning is the life of God in the heart. When Jesus said to the scribe, "Thou art not far from the kingdom" (Mark 12:34), this was what he meant. You are not far from life—real life—life abundant! Life eternal!

Said Canon Peter Green of Manchester, "There is no emotion so necessary to a true religion, nor any so fundamental to it, as the sense of belonging to God." I fear we are getting away from this sense of belonging in our modern world and church. To be sure, it is nice to be moral. Attending worship services now and again is the proper thing. Join a church if you like, providing the demands are not too stringent. Even serve in an official capacity if it doesn't break in upon your leisure. But "belong to God"? Careful now! Let us not be too intimate in our faith.

Yet, I say again, this personal relationship is primary to all ethical and spiritual experiences. Jesus did not say to Nicodemus, *"All* the Jews must join in the fraternity of the redeemed." To be sure, he wanted it so. But he said to this brilliant teacher, *"Ye* must be born again" (John 3:7).

Here is an old hymn. We do not sing it very often but that does not keep it from being true.

> Tis done: the great transaction's done!
> I am my Lord's and he is mine;

He drew me and I followed on,
Charmed to confess the voice divine.[1]

But "the kingdom is at hand" is not only personal. It is social. In fact, when our Lord stated it, it was as a public declaration. It is the experience of God in the heart. It is also very definitely the expression of God in the world.

"Thy kingdom come," our Lord taught us to pray, and he continued, "Thy will be done on *earth*." So! it is the coming of God to the life. But it is more. It is the continuance of God through the land.

The seer of Patmos heard heavenly voices declare, "The kingdoms of this world are become the kingdoms of our Lord" (Rev. 11:15). This does not necessarily mean some far-off event. There are genuine revivals taking place in our world today. There are spirit movements that are unquestionably real. In Japan recently, thousands of men and women have become Christians as a result of stirring evangelistic efforts. It is not correct to think that the New Testament kingdom refers *only* to heaven, and I say that as one who believes in the afterlife. Jesus said, "This is life eternal, that they might know thee the only true God, and Jesus Christ, whom thou hast sent" (John 17:3). Not will be, but is—not will know, but know.

It is also an incorrect assumption that the kingdom is reserved only for a select group. God had been tremendously patient with Simon in proving this point. What a great

[1] Philip Doddridge, "O Happy Day That Fixed My Choice."

day it was for the big fisherman when he was able in his own heart to say with conviction, "Whosoever believeth in him shall receive remission of sins" (Acts 10:43).

I am much in sympathy with that bit of doggerel that is aptly and sarcastically used by Dr. William Barclay in one of his books:

> We are God's chosen few,
>   All others will be damned;
> There is no room in heaven for you—
>   We can't have heaven crammed.[2]

I am not sure but that if one believes that, he is in greater need of salvation than one who is entirely oblivious to the claims of Christ.

III

"Repent."

The first two imperatives are declarations: "The time is fulfilled." "The kingdom is at hand." The last two imperatives are commands: "Repent." "Believe." For mark you, if one responds at the appointed hour to the anointed king he is under orders of the new regime. And the first command issued is, "Repent."

Now repentance means to change one's mind—his heart. However, this order cannot be fulfilled, this command cannot be carried out, unless two things happen.

First, there must be a *dissatisfaction* for what one has

[2] *Flesh and Spirit* (Nashville: Abingdon Press, 1962), p. 72.

been. Jesus knew there was no use in calling men to the new life if they were satisfied with the old. You can never start toward Canaan if you keep Egypt in your heart. That lonely lost boy of whom Jesus spoke would never have longed for home if he had been contented with the hogs.

Somehow when the Lord Christ comes our way the things which once seemed so important do not really matter at all. I wonder what happened to the water jar that the woman of Sychar brought to the well that day. I wonder who moved into Matthew's vacated office when the tax collector gave up his business. Had one walked down near the harbor in Capernaum after Jesus had preached there one day, he might have noticed a sign which read, "Used boats for sale." I wonder who bought them.

We will never know the answers to those thoughts, but we do know what happened to the woman and Matthew and the fishermen. They were dissatisfied with life as they had lived it in the light of his higher call.

The second thing is there must be a *dedication* to what one can be. The boy we spoke of, who was companioning with the hogs, learned this. "I perish with hunger" was not enough. "I will go to my father" was what restored the relationship. "I perish" must always lead to "I go" if the longing soul finds its home.

This, I think, is the most significant fact of the Christian quest. Genuine consecration does not depend on how many of our sins we confess but how much of ourselves we commit.

This is why our Lord could answer John the Baptist's invitation to be baptized with water unto repentance. He did not have a guilty past to regret. But he did have a great future to dedicate. This, I repeat, is the very heart of the gospel.

IV

"Believe the gospel." This is the second command.

"The time is fulfilled" and "the Kingdom is at hand" have been declared unto us. "Repent," we have been commanded. Look at the past with dissatisfaction—look toward the future with dedication.

Now says our Lord, "Believe the gospel—the good news." That is, since the hour is here and the king has come, and you have not been satisfied with what has gone before but are looking eagerly toward a future made radiant with his presence, rest your life in his will. Ally yourself with this faith!

I think it is of great moment to note that as soon as our Lord issued this second order he began calling men to his side and his service: "Come ye after *me*, and I will make you to become fishers of men" (Mark 1:17). I take it then that whatever believing the good news means, it certainly means this: shouldering his banner and sharing his truth.

Dr. Fosdick is right when he affirms, "Jesus did not say, 'Worship me'; he said, 'Follow me.' A great soul does not want his ego idolized; he wants his cause supported."

Are you willing to follow? Are you willing to fish? There

is a world before us and people who are lonely and lost and filled with fear. Some of them do not know what it is they need, but it is God's good news. Will you give yourself to him and then take the good news to them?

Some days ago it was my great privilege to see a man enter the gates of new life for the first time. He was a man of mature years who was so utterly and joyously transformed he could scarcely believe it himself. "O to think," he said, "I have had the opportunity all my life to accept Christ. If only I had known what I was missing."

For you, for others, he now requests your acceptance. This is life at its best. This is why you were born. Don't miss it!

A VALIANT FAITH

For I am not ashamed of the gospel of Christ: for it is the power of God unto salvation to every one that believeth; to the Jew first, and also to the Greek. (Rom. 1:16.)

It may be a momentous thing for one to assert dogmatically that he is not ashamed. Yet it is often necessary for a sense of shame to serve as a kind of doorway into meaningful and worthwhile adventures.

Here, for instance, is a young nobleman standing at the threshold of high usefulness. He will one day become the prophetic power of Jerusalem. When social reformers are named, this ardent advocate of God's righteousness will lead the list. What, however, preceded this ministry of so great import? Listen to his own words: "Woe is me! for I am undone; because I am a man of unclean lips" (Isa. 6:5). Thus, this experience became the entrance to vast significance.

But if shame may serve as a guide to good, it may also be a block to bad. An embarrassed conscience may indeed be a fitting post of warning. Another has suggested that a blush is the red flag modesty hangs above the citadel of the soul.

Remembering his home and how he had disgraced it perhaps helped the prodigal boy more than any other thing to close the door on the evil of the far country.

A young soldier overseas nearly bartered virtue for vice but his integrity won out. "I don't know what kept me from slipping," he said, "unless it was a friend I remembered back home. I was ashamed to do what I was about to do when I thought of the hurt it would bring him."

Having considered briefly this truth, let us look at three questions that appear significant.

I

Of what was Paul not ashamed? "I am not ashamed of the gospel of Christ" is his answer.

The gospel to Paul, it would seem, had two dominating principles. The first was *God's action*. This is the primary premise of the Roman epistle. Listen to the apostle at this point: "If God is for us, who is against us?" "God has done what the law could not do." "The gift of God is eternal life." "God shows his love for us." Or view afresh these phrases that are found throughout the letter: God's decree, God's kindness, God's truthfulness, God's righteousness.

The stress that Paul placed upon the Eternal in this particular letter was certainly not new for the evangelist. When the way was difficult God was the one to whom he looked. When gratitude welled up within his heart, as it did constantly, he gave thanks to God. When he left a church and departed on another pilgrimage he placed the flock in God's care.

If you suggest that to be reminded of this fact is childishly elementary, I can only answer that we are failing to give this fact its preeminent position in our modern theology.

We sing, "Lord, we are able," but then read in the Gospel of Mark, "They [the disciples] all forsook him, and fled" (Mark 14:50). We preach, "Let us build the kingdom," forgetting that the Master said, "It is your Father's good pleasure to give you the kingdom" (Luke 12:32), as if the kingdom of God were an edifice to be raised instead of an experience to be received.

I submit that it is more than the tune that gives "How Great Thou Art" its place of distinction in our church music. It puts the emphasis exactly where it merits attention —not on us but God!

But the gospel for Paul would not only include God's action but also *man's reception*—what a man in Christ will do with and for the good news.

This is an all-pervading concept of Paul. The evangelist is tremendously concerned with the conduct people must keep, the striving they must do, the witness they must share, and the account they must give. The action ethic permeates his writings as leaven does the lump.

Emil Brunner, in *Man in Revolt,* is concerned that we catch the wholesomeness of such thinking. He writes, "Faith in Jesus Christ is not an interpretation of the world, but it is participation in an event."

And, of course, it is—in all areas. If God's hand is reaching out to bestow his countless blessings and especially his gift of salvation, then my hand must be reaching out to receive. Not only so, but my hand must be employed in the task of rekindling—keeping aglow that gift, as Paul reminded young Timothy. Then we must be channels for this blessing. Paul told the Ephesian church that salvation was the gift of God. But in the very next breath, he says we are "created in Christ Jesus unto good works" (Eph. 2:10).

What can this mean if it does not mean we are to be sharers of such mercy?

II

Why was it that Paul was not ashamed of the gospel? "It is the power of God unto salvation." Let us observe how the apostle defined this good news. Notice, in the first place, he does not say the gospel is *intellectual force*. To be sure, Paul does not bypass mental effort. "I beseech you therefore, brethren, by the mercies of God, that ye present your bodies a living sacrifice, holy, acceptable unto God, which is your reasonable service. . . . Be ye transformed by the renewing of your mind," he said to this group of followers (Rom. 12:1-2). And "I would not have you ignorant" could be taken out of context and rightly called not simply a statement made to the Corinthians and Thessalonians but his constant conviction and attitude toward all the churches he loved.

But good news is more. It is intelligence plus. You may remember what the little country woman said to the learned guest who came to preach in her small rural church. His degrees required as much room on the Sunday bulletin as his name and sermon topic. However, after his brilliant dissertation failed to lift her spiritually, her terse comment was, "Son, it don't do no good to have the pedigree unless you got the horse."

If Paul did not define the gospel as an intellectual force, neither did he declare it to be a *strict law*. Knowing people as he did, he knew there would be disagreements as to how religion should be practiced. He had seen churches quibble and quarrel over the smallest items of religious customs. He did not want the young sensitive fellowship in Rome to make that mistake. Listen to his counsel concerning one particular: "He is not a Jew, which is one outwardly; neither is that circumcision, which is outward in the flesh: But he is a Jew, which is one inwardly; and circumcision, is that of the heart, in the spirit, and not in the letter" (Rom. 2:28-29).

And again he says, "By the deeds of the law there shall no flesh be justified in his sight: for by the law is the knowledge of sin" (Rom. 3:20).

Then, for Paul, the gospel is not a matter of *human effort*. We have agreed that man must cooperate by receiving what God is constantly seeking to give, but growth in

33

Christ is not dependent so much on striving as it is surrendering. The power to mature spiritually is ours only through the unmerited grace of the Father. The apostle in speaking of how a man arrives in Christ-like fruition says, "It is not a question of human will or effort but of the divine mercy" (Rom. 9:16 Moffatt).

I well remember one night in the company of a dear friend seeking to lead a youth to Christ. This young man was having a difficult time both seeing and starting the way. My friend was deeply interested in the one we were seeking to win for the kingdom. Finally, after we had failed in several approaches, he said to him, "Jim, just stop trying and start trusting." He had hardly gotten the words out of his mouth when the new day dawned. So! entering the gates of new life is contingent first upon our assurance, not our activity. Our confidence in him generally precedes our communion with him and our commission for him.

If the gospel then is not intellectual force, strict law, and human effort, what is it? Says the apostle, "It is God's saving power." Thus explaining simply the meaning of the gospel, Paul is in complete agreement with his Lord as to the purpose of his coming. Consider the words of another: "Christ was a teacher but one never hears of his being called 'Professor.' He was a healer but he is not referred to as 'Doctor.' He was a preacher but no one ever speaks of him as 'the Reverend.' 'The Son of man came to save the lost,' Jesus said. (Luke 19:10 RSV) We must know him as Savior."

Our modern wording may be different. As we seek to describe a panacea for our problems, one may say he requires psychoanalysis. One may suggest the remedy for his ills is therapeutic medicine. Another may affirm the answer to his need is integration of personality. But whatever the phrasing, our weakened, warring, wayward humanity awakes each morning on the brink of some new hell and cries out with the Philippian jailer, "What must I do to be saved?" (Acts 16:30.)

III

To whom was this gospel Paul unashamedly declared to be presented?

"To every one that believeth"; Paul answers, "to the Jew first, and also to the Greek."

He longed, in the first place, for the Jews to find *renewal*. Here is a good twentieth-century word that needs to be explained and experienced across our church. If Dr. Samuel Johnson were correct in avowing that most people need not so much to be told (for the first time) as reminded, then we can certainly apply his words to this instance.

"Still, by way of refreshing your memory," Paul says to the Roman church, "I have written to you with a certain freedom" (Rom. 15:15 Moffatt). There are a number of abiding essentials to which the apostle refers that are timely and timeless in their task of giving spiritual growth.

There is simple faith in Jesus Christ. How it must have staggered the Jewish mind to hear his voice declaring that righteousness is not of the law but that it comes through confidence in Christ. (Rom. 3:21-22.) Christ's emphasis was not law but life, not outer rules but inner righteousness, not regulated programs but redeemed people.

Then he mentions peace. This peace came as a result of faith in Christ. (Rom. 5:1.) In our day peace is a retreat we seek. For Paul it was a victory to share. (Rom. 5:2.) How often do we preach peace as something passive —a fruit of virtuous living? How seldom do we preach peace as something active—a fact of Christian witness?

Certainly peace is the calm of a committed life. It is one of those blessed added attractions of the gospel. But the main purpose of peace within is to give us passion without that we may declare that justification of which Paul speaks to all men.

Genuine concern for others is expressed. Would you like to know how deep this went with Paul? "I could wish that myself were accursed from Christ for my brethren." (Rom. 9:3.) There is nothing superficial about a soul-interest like that!

Like his Lord Paul found opposition at this point. It was the conviction of the evangelist from Tarsus that both Jew and Gentile needed to be saved. The Greeks needed to be converted from their foul deeds and the Jews from their false creeds. Paul preached that there was no difference in the sight of God toward these two groups and that Christ would redeem both. (Rom. 10:12-13.)

In the second place, Paul knew that if the Jews needed renewal, the Gentiles needed *redemption*. He had seen churches move from the center to the circumference. He wanted the Jews to cling fast to its cardinal principles.

But in order that Jew and Greek be united in the faith, Paul knew that these Greeks had to do two things. There had to be a turning from and a facing toward; they had not only to repent but respond.

Now they had deteriorated to the extent that not only were they worshiping pagan shrines but even birds and reptiles. Paul reminds them of the forbearance and patience of God, but he also reminds them that God's kindness is meant to guide them to repentance. They must literally change their minds concerning the altar of supreme devotion.

There are members in the church today who have never changed their minds and yielded their highest allegiances to Christ. To be sure, there are no pagan shrines in their living rooms. One could search through the entire section of our neighborhood and find no heathen totem being venerated. And yet money, business, status, even one's family may be revered to the extent that the kingdom is ignored and the Christ betrayed. How great our need to repent!

But repenting must lead to responding. You must indeed "present your bodies." This will bring life from the dead, says Paul. How this Jew loved these Gentiles. "I am a missionary to the Gentiles," he writes. And how deeply he yearned for them to make this offering, this response to God.

A layman who is one of my dearest friends was transformed by Christ. From spending much of his life in jail he became an earnest Christian. "Ed," I asked, "what made you change your direction?" "Wallace," he answered, "if Jesus could walk up a hill for me, I figured I could walk down an aisle for him." It is a walk which is continuing, for he is now the lay leader of his church and a power for good in his community.

Listen to Paul tell about his own reaction to Jesus that day on the Damascus Road: "I was not disobedient unto the heavenly vision" (Acts 26:19).

This is the response that redeems. And what it did for Paul and the Gentiles, this same commitment will do for the church now if we are willing to make it.

THREE CHEERS

*I have told you this so that you can share
my joy, and that your happiness may be complete. (John 15:11 Phillips.)*

I am glad that Jesus used the phrase "my joy." If any
man had it, he did. One unforgettable thing that impresses
even the most casual reader of the New Testament is the
amazing gladness of our Lord. One might even say that it
was his most distinctive characteristic next to his commitment to the Father. The two, however, cannot be separated.
Joy sprang from his dedication as water flows from a spring.

His enemies noticed his great zest for living and exclaimed, "Behold a man gluttonous" (Matt. 11:19). Jesus
might have answered this accusation with a statement made
elsewhere: "My meat is to do the will of him that sent
me" (John 4:34).

We have said his joy came from his dedication. Actually
this was what he was saying in the words chosen for our
text. "I have told you *this* so that you can share my joy."
This refers, of course, to what he had been saying to them
immediately before. And that particular subject was his
relationship to the Father.

Now if Jesus wanted his disciples to share his joy as he

suggests in our text, where can we look for the source of such happiness? On at least three occasions Jesus offered men good cheer, that glad encouragement he alone can give.

I

The first occasion was when he offered *the cheer of his divine forgiveness.*

The incident takes place in Capernaum. A man was paralyzed. Some of his friends, having heard of Jesus, placed him on a rug and brought him to the Master. Then we hear his lifting words, "Son, be of good cheer; thy sins be forgiven thee" (Matt. 9:2). Oh, the joyful confidence of this command!

However, this mandate brought little delight to the scribes. "This man is blaspheming," they said. No doubt Capernaum had its miracle workers. But the city was short on its sin-forgivers. This was the task of God alone, and of course they did not hold to the idea of Jesus' divinity. Thus denying his privilege to pardon, they were at the same time denying his union with the Father. To be sure, forgiveness is the task of God. But Jesus is God.

Do you remember the story of the kindly priest who was making the rounds in the hospital? He came to a ward where death hovered near an elderly saint. For more than sixty years she had been on a pilgrimage to the city where there is no night. "Good morning," he said graciously; "I have come to grant you absolution." "I'm sorry," she answered, "I do not understand what you mean." "I have come to forgive your sins," he explained. "May I see your hands," she questioned. Somewhat puzzled he held out his hands. "You cannot do it," she exclaimed earnestly; "the One who forgives my sins has nail-pierced hands."

"He is not the one who can," says the doubter. "He is the only one who can," says the delivered. So the service ended. The scribes went home scoffing, and the man went home saved.

Certainly his affliction was cured, but more important his sin was forgiven. In all probability his illness had been caused by a dissipated life.

"Be of good cheer; thy sins be forgiven." That is the great need today in our world. There is no problem that sin has not caused. There is no difficulty that forgiveness cannot remedy.

Then I am persuaded it is the great need in our church. How few of us seem to really be of good cheer. What a small number actually live as if the courageous gladness of God had filled every bit of their hearts.

Alistair MacLean, the Highland Shepherd, was right. People should stop and stare because of the very radiance on the face of one who walks with the Redeemer.

When Moses came down from Mount Sinai we read that "his face was in a glow after speaking to God." I want this glory to crown my experience. It is possible through his grace for us all to share such splendor.

We may not all possess the capacity to teach in a class, sing in a choir, stand in a pulpit, or preside in a conference.

But the sons and daughters of the King who are the church eternal have been the ones with gladdened souls that gave to this earth glowing faces.

After all, our Lord did not say, "You are the skilled of mankind." Neither did he say, "You are the talented of humanity." He said, "You are the light of the world."

II

The second instance was when he offered *the cheer of his unfailing presence*.

This particular scene occurs after Jesus had been preaching to the multitude and healing the sick near the plain of Gennesaret.

No doubt he was tired. Perhaps he felt mentally and spiritually drained and in need of that renewing energy he received constantly from his Father. So after compelling the disciples to get in their boat and face toward Bethsaida, he went up into the hills to pray.

A few hours later a storm came. Knowing the smallness of the boat in comparison to the lake and also knowing the smallness of some men's courage in the midst of what must have been a terrific storm, his great heart would not let them endure it alone. Across the waters he walked out to join them. At first they were fearful, imagining him to be a ghost. But he calmed them as afterward he calmed the turbulent sea. Here are his words: "Be of good cheer; it is I; be not afraid" (Matt. 14:27).

This bracing news is just as relevant today and just as

essential as when our Lord shared it on the Galilean sea. What storms have you not faced, will you not face in the not too distant future? What howling winds and rising waves have I not known, will I not know in the immediate tomorrows? What crisis hours have we not passed through, will we not pass through before the night is passed and the sea is still?

I well remember my own journey to the Galilean coasts. The weather is quite unpredictable. It would be clear at one moment and without warning a storm would fall upon us. So in many lives. It may be the sudden storm that results in the death of one whom we love dearly. It may be the storm of an incurable disease that places its merciless fingers like a yoke about our necks. It may be the storm of unrealized dreams, to "watch the things you gave your life to broken." Then it is that the truth of this mighty story comes like the dawn after the dark. For the disciples' need is, after all, our need—not a stronger boat but a steady hand; not the absence of a storm but the presence of a Saviour; not a calm lake but a committed life.

Notice when he came. We read in Matthew during the "fourth watch of the night"; that is, just before daylight, and is not that often the darkest hour? But, you see, that is when we need him most.

Dr. Weatherhead tells about a boy who was fatally injured on the battlefield. His closest friend saw him fall and started out from his trench across no-man's-land to give him aid. Warned by those about him in the furrow that there was no use, he still crawled out across the plain to his friend and somehow managed to get him back to the trench. In doing this, however, he was mortally injured while his friend was dead. Someone exclaimed that it was not worth it. "But it was worth it," he responded. "When I got to him he was still alive and he said to me, 'Jim, I knew you'd come.'"

There is an even greater friend than that. Listen to what Moses says about him. "Be strong and of a good courage, fear not . . . for the Lord thy God will not fail thee, nor forsake thee." (Deut. 31:6.) If that is not enough to cheer, what would it take?

III

The last example we shall mention is when Jesus offered *the cheer of his eternal power*.

This scene takes place in the Upper Room. The Gospel of John does not mention the last supper as do the other three Gospels. Instead, John relates how our Lord washed the feet of the disciples.

There has been constant bickering across the years concerning these two incidents as they have been compared. Some have suggested that only one of them actually took place. Others have sought to show the preeminence of one over the other.

I think both of them speak to our hearts and tenderly reveal his heart. We cannot, we must not, dismiss either experience. In one version he anticipates the death of a martyr. In the other, he illustrates the duty of a disciple. In one version he shared a supper so they would not cease remembering his passion. In the other, he shared a towel so they would not cease revealing his mission. In one version he is Saviour. In the other he is servant. Can there be one without the other? For he said, "The Son of man has come . . . to . . . save," and again, "The Son of man has . . . come . . . to serve" (Luke 19:10; Matt. 20:28 Moffatt).

There follows then his intimate words concerning the coming of the Holy Spirit and their relationship to him. He next discusses their attitude toward the world and the unfailing resources available for their needs. We come now to the words of our final point: "In the world ye shall have tribulation: but be of good cheer; I have overcome the world" (John 16:33).

"How presumptuous," say his critics. "Overcome the world, indeed. In the very next scene he is arrested. Did he overcome the soldiers? He is then tried as a common criminal. Did he overcome the governor? Finally, he is led captive to the top of a hill where he dies a despicable death. Did he overcome the cross?"

Well, look again at these tremendous hours and judge for yourself.

When one of the mob in the garden had lost his ear by the sword of impulsive Simon, Jesus healed the man and said, "Put your sword into its sheath; shall I not drink the cup which the Father has given me?" I ask you now, does that sound like a man groveling at the feet of his captors?

Stand with him in the praetorium. Yes, he is the one on trial, but look at Pilate. See him nervously examine his prisoner. Watch as in great agitation he seeks his release. Finally, see him as he cowardly washes his hands. You would think it is the other man who is the accused. Not once throughout the entire trial does our Lord lose his composure or become flustered.

So to Calvary. And the mob has its day and the foes of darkness their hour. "It is finished," he says. The Jews can breathe easily now—the great Disturber is no more. His friends will be less embarrassed now—their kinsman who was "out of his mind" is gone. His closest disciples will be less constrained now—the beautiful dream of a kingdom where all men are brothers is over.

But three days later: the stone is gone; the grave is empty; the Christ is alive! "All power in heaven and on earth has been given to me," he claims and breathes upon them the Holy Spirit. Thus clothed in that power, the disciples begin their witness that shall not stop with Jerusalem and Judea and Samaria, but shall eventually lead to the ends of the earth. No wonder John could say our faith in him results in "victory that overcometh the world" (I John 5:4).

"What does faith mean to you," E. Stanley Jones once asked a Hindu who had recently become a Christian. "Victory," he answered, "over sin and self and fear of death. My faith means these three things: Victory! Victory! Victory!" [1]

Christ had this victorious power in the shadow of the Cross. The disciples had it as they claimed the world in his name. The transformed Hindu had it so that he was able to testify without fear.

So be of good cheer, of glad encouragement. Your sins are forgiven. The Lord is your companion. He has overcome the world. The victory is yours to claim. It is yours to keep. It is yours to share!

[1] I am indebted to Dr. Norman Paullin for this story.

THE POWER OF PRAISE

At midnight Paul and Silas prayed, and
sang praises unto God. (Acts 16:25.)

This to me is one of the great scenes of the New Testament. Of course, Paul and Silas were not unlike thousands of Christians who belonged to the early church and sang their way through the persecutions that befell them. One of the amazing glories of all history is the way those brave followers of the faith with courageous souls and singing hearts channeled the glow that lighted the world.

> "Dead men tell no tales!" they chuckled,
>   As the singing saviors died,
> A few serene, and many shackled,
>   Scourged, tortured, crucified.[1]

Yet it was with their very songs that these "singing saviors," these witnesses of the way, revealed the greatness of God and the grace of Jesus Christ. It is rather difficult not to believe in a thing when one watches men persecuted yet proclaiming God's praises. Now we do not have to

[1] Clement Wood, "The Singing Saviors," used by permission of Mrs. Gloria Goddard Wood.

depend solely upon the history of the Christian church for this expression of inner victory. To be sure, there is sufficient evidence here to declare its merit. But the singing soul has always been a part of our religious heritage.

Early in the Old Testament we hear Moses declaring, "The Lord is my song" (Exod. 15:2). The theme of much of our psalter is: "Praise ye the Lord: for it is good to sing praises unto our God" (Ps. 147:1).

The church fathers did not feel the Bible could end without a great hymn of praise, so we read in Revelation that the song of the Lamb was sung glorifying his marvelous works. (Rev. 15:3.)

This mighty truth leaps at us, too, from the Gospels. It is indeed significant to observe that the Gospels open with a hallelujah chorus praising Christ's birth! (Luke 2: 13.) Then as Mark nears the close of his book with our Lord facing Calvary, he writes that they left the Upper Room with a hymn on their lips (Mark 14:26), and no doubt this was a hymn of praise.

It would seem then that singing praises is of tremendous significance in the continued revelation of God.

Let us look with new interest at this scene from which our text is taken.

I

Note in the first place where Paul and Silas sang—"in prison." Luke tells us they were cast into the "inner prison." Now no doubt this was more of a dungeon than a jail, thus denoting its location underground. In all probability there was little air and less light. Then Luke reminds us that their feet were made fast "in the stocks." That is, their feet were pressed through small openings in wood and, of course, securely fastened. This not only held them tightly but was an added agony.

Now when men sing in such an environment as that, it has to be because they have a victorious melody in their hearts.

It was my distinct privilege recently to be associated in an Evangelistic Mission with Martin Niemöller. This great ambassador of the king had spent many weary months in prison because of his refusal to sanction the principles of Hitler. One afternoon as we were walking together, he said something to me that I have never forgotten. He is a very modest man and there was not the slightest trace of pride in his tone. We were but discussing the convictions he had which he refused to cast aside. "There was never a time," he testified, "even in the darkest hours, that I was tempted to give up the faith."

When I think of this humble, courageous disciple whom all German Christians and world Christians stand and salute, and when I reflect upon the music of his soul that even the Nazi prisons could not hush, I want to proclaim triumphantly not only, "What a man he is," but, "What a Master he has!"

And that is how I feel when I read of this incident at Philippi. Paul and Silas were dragged to the public square.

The magistrates ordered the police to beat them with rods. Luke reports that "they laid many stripes upon them." Then to prison and the stocks.

How easy it would have been then to have thrown in the towel. Had they not come to the Roman colony of Philippi under God's guidance? Had they not touched a slave girl who was mentally ill and restored her to normalcy? For this they were flogged, imprisoned, and tortured. I say lesser men would have groveled in self-pity: "Why should this have happened to us?" But not so with Paul and Silas. They began to sing and glorify the Lord. Even the agnostic mind looking at this dungeon scene has to admit there must be something in a man's heart that will cause his voice to ring out in exaltation when he is in prison stocks.

II

Note in the second place when Paul and Silas sang—"at midnight." It would be well for us to picture this scene in our minds so as to clearly view this amazing incident.

These men had been stripped and beaten with rods. It was not out of the ordinary for such punishment to be fatal. The Jews never gave a prisoner more than thirty-nine lashes. The Romans, however, gave as many as they wished. Perhaps Paul had this very beating in mind when later in writing to the Corinthians he uses the phrase "stripes above measure."

The first thing the Philippian jailer did after being saved

was to care for the marks on the men's backs. Even before he was baptized he washed their wounds.

But this is after. No soothing balm has yet been poured on their bruises. The pain has not ceased. The stocks do not allow them even to lie flat on their stomachs seeking some degree of comfort. The midnight darkness has engulfed them. Then it is that they began to sing. Luke says that first they prayed. So! as a result of trusting there came singing. The seeking for his Spirit led to the praises for his presence. These weary, battered, fastened men could sing because of the companionship of one who makes yokes easy and burdens light. (Matt. 11:30.)

Yes, the pain was still felt; the suffering was still real; the night was still dark. But he was there. "Come unto me," he said, "take my yoke . . . and ye shall find rest unto your souls" (Matt. 11:28-29). My soul! No wonder the anthem pealed forth. No one but Jesus can give music at midnight!

This is one of the great glories of our gospel. One of the Old Testament sages found that his way was often quite dark. But his path to praise began when he remembered that "in the night his song shall be with me."

Have you ever learned the secret of the song in the night? The darkness may be upon you. Some day soon, perhaps even now, you are in the midst of midnight. Of course, you may not be confined in prison but you are behind bars just as confining.

You may be in the grip of some incurable disease. Listen

to one who knows such an illness: "I have learned to thank God for my cancer; it has brought me close to him."

Sorrow may have come and covered your life with a veil of shadows. Think of these words from a young husband whose wife's death caused him unspeakable anguish: "In my bewilderment at being unable to find her hand I found his hand, and in that grip I can face the future with confidence."

Temptation may be causing you moments of frustration and despair. Here is a statement made by a lad that I feel cannot be improved upon: "Whenever evil knocks at my door, I ask the Master to answer." In the darkest hours these hearts have learned to sing.

III

Finally, observe what Paul and Silas sang—"praises." Of course, this point has already been anticipated, even considered, as it has had to be in the light of the total context of the story.

Yet, the amazement never ceases. A dirge perhaps, a mournful lament, but singing praises? Men held fast in the stocks, nursing bleeding wounds, at the midnight hour bursting forth with hymns of praise? Do you see why I dared suggest at the beginning that this is one of the great scenes of the New Testament?

I don't know which of the psalms these men sang in the Philippian dungeon that night. There are some great hymns of praise in the Old Testament. Somehow I doubt really if the words were very important. The fact that they lifted their voices in exultation—that is the big point!

One night, years ago, our ship docked at the harbor in Yokohama. The barge was carrying a group of us from the steamer to the immigration bureau. There was a strange mixture on that barge: men of all stations from many countries. Most of them were men of low estate. I recall that there was much obscene language used by those whose words we could understand. Another minister shared my company and we began to sing a hymn of praise. I do not recall all the words we sang. And I am very certain we were not prize choristers. But explain it how you will, the profanity ceased and even the most boisterous of the lot grew still.

Many insist that praying makes a difference. Well, so does praising!

When the singing ended, Luke tells us that an earthquake followed. There is little doubt but that God was on the scene. Are we not told earlier in Acts that when the disciples prayed "the place was shaken where they were assembled"?

Realizing the power of God at work, the keeper of the prison asked these men the question that millions have since asked: "What must I do to be saved?" When the word of the Lord had been spoken to him, Luke says he "rejoiced, believing in God with all his house." Thus the primary result of these two men praising God was not the earthquake in Philippi but the earthquake in the heart of the Philippian jailer. These stripes which he had not been concerned about, perhaps had helped inflict, he now washed. These prisoners he had punished, he now fed. The Christ to whom he had been so indifferent, he now admitted into his life and served him with his actions.

It is an old story, that of the forty gallant men in the Roman army who became Christians. These men sang about their faith:

> Forty wrestlers—wrestling for thee, O Christ—
> For thee we claim the victory,
> For thee we claim the crown.

Sempronius, the centurion, received the edict where his army was encamped, proclaiming that Caesar was a god and that every man must burn incense before this decree. The forty men declared that they paid homage to only one God. The captain then ordered that they strip themselves of their uniforms and march out into the freezing night to die. As they marched, they sang:

> Forty wrestlers—wrestling for thee, O Christ—
> For thee we claim the victory,
> For thee we claim the crown.

Sempronius listened, astonished at such devotion. After a bit, however, the singing stopped. The officer stood at his station for a moment and then a slinking, shivering soldier was seen moving with shaking fingers to burn incense before the edict.

Sempronius knew then why the men had ceased their chorus. They numbered only thirty-nine. For a few moments all was quiet; then suddenly across the frozen fields there came the sound of song. But there seemed to be a new joy and a fresh enthusiasm in the music.

> Forty wrestlers—wrestling for thee, O Christ—
> For thee we claim the victory,
> For thee, we claim the crown.

It was Sempronius, their captain, who was singing with them. What power, praise!

DIVINE PROMISES

Every promise of God finds its affirmative in him [Christ]. (II Cor. 1:20 Phillips.)

Here is a word from Paul that brings with it the light of morning and the kiss of spring. How this refreshing declaration must have brought hope and heart to the Christian community at Corinth.

Corinth was the most populous city in Greece. It was not only a principal Roman trade center, but it was the capital of the province of Achaia. But it was a wicked city that was in desperate need of Christian witness. Here then was this encouraging news from Paul. The pledges that God gave to Israel are now valid in his Son. Every promise of God has become true in Christ.

Do you see what this means? There is no need now to continue searching and seeking and striving to find an answer for the world's questions or a solution for this life's problems. He is here! Of course, evil is still about us. Sin still exists. But the way to overcome is available. Yes, and the Person to whom we can point those who are evil and sinful is present.

We read in the pages of the Old Testament, "I will never

break my covenant with you" (Judg. 2:1). The Lord has kept faith. He has not forgotten his agreements. "Every promise of God finds [has found] its affirmative in him."

Let us look at some of these promises and see how they have been fulfilled, how they have become true, in Christ.

I

"The Lord . . . shall give you a sign; Behold, a virgin shall conceive, and bear a son, and shall call his name Immanuel." (Isa. 7:14.) The first promise to which we shall devote our interest is this: Immanuel—God is with us. Christ is *the presence of God.*

I must admit my deep animosity for that part of the doctrine of humanism that denies the divinity of Jesus Christ. There are those, I know, who look at Jesus' words, "I and my Father are one" (John 10:30) and answer, "Oh, certainly, but so is it true that all are one with God who are in sympathy with his principles and dedicated to their practices."

But are you in a position, indeed, do you know anyone who is in a position worthy of declaring, "He that hath seen me hath seen the Father"?

It has been my great joy and blessing to meet some truly marvelous souls that I have considered saints: that amazing Japanese Christian, Toyohiko Kagawa; the German spiritual leader, Martin Niemöller; American missionary, Stanley Jones. I earnestly believe you would have to do considerable surveying before you would find men more committed than

58

these three. But I never heard one of them say, "He that hath seen me hath seen the Father."

This then is the place where the unique character of our Lord is evident. Few theologians have exerted more influence in the twentieth century than Rudolf Bultmann. Notice his attitude at this point: "When Jesus speaks, we hear the word of God."

So! he is the presence of God. And that presence never fails nor forsakes. "I will be with thee," says the God of the Old Testament (Josh. 1:5). "I am with you alway," says the Christ of the New (Matt. 28:20).

I heard Olin Stockwell, who was a prisoner in Red China, tell an inspiring incident. When the Communists first came in, one of the persons they apprehended was a young Christian. It was months before Stockwell had a communication from him. Then a letter came saying he was alive and that he was writing to inform him that he was in a prison camp some distance away. Under his signature was one word: Immanuel. It was a word the Communists could not translate. But the missionary knew its meaning and its relevance. Christ was with him!

I think that is what Paul felt when he wrote, "The Lord stood with me, and strengthened me" (II Tim. 4:17).

II

"I will also give thee for a light to the Gentiles, that thou mayest be my salvation unto the end of the earth."

(Isa. 49:6.) Here is the second promise Jesus fulfilled. He is *the Saviour of men*.

There are two particular points that need our comprehension under this heading. The first is the *office* of Christ. He himself said, "The Son of man is come . . . to save" (Luke 19:10).

Now there are those who do not feel their need for redemption and some are decent respectable folk. They consider the new birth to be something that the moral wastrel is sadly lacking. But intelligence or culture or philanthropy has made them part of a select group. Smug in their own repute, they live lacking nothing.

Yet we must remember that Jesus was not speaking to a derelict or a degenerate or a drunkard when he said, "Ye must be born again" (John 3:7). He was talking to a man who was wealthy, intelligent, and religious. But Nicodemus was missing the one thing that he needed: the receiving of Christ in return for the giving of himself. And this is the new birth—the salvation our Lord yearns to give.

A brilliant gentleman said to me recently, "Mr. Chappell, you lay too much stress on Christ our Saviour and not enough on Jesus our Example." My reply was, "The best example of him I know is that he is our Saviour."

As we think of our Lord as the Saviour of men, I feel it is urgent not only to see the office of Christ but the *outreach* of Christ. "Unto the end of the earth," reads the prophecy. "To save that which was lost," said the Saviour. Our gospel is for all men or it is not for any man.

Look again at those to whom he opened the gates of the kingdom. We spoke of Nicodemus who was a member of the Sanhedrin. There was also a crucified revolutionist. The point is that every man was encompassed in the sphere of his affection.

"Which of your children do you love the best," one asked a mother with a large family. I considered her answer beautifully significant. "I love the sick until he is well and the lost one until he is found," she replied.

God has children in need. Some are black and yellow and red. Some are poor and wretched and maimed. Is God's salvation and love and care working through us to bring them the promised Messiah?

III

"For unto us a child is born, unto us a son is given . . . and his name shall be called The Prince of Peace." (Isa. 9:6.) The third promise we shall observe is the fulfillment of this great prophecy. Christ is *the prince of peace*.

It matters little to me whether you think the prophet was anticipating an immediate leader, a rising national power, or a coming Messiah. The fact is that Jesus Christ so wonderfully manifested this inspired declaration that even the critics of this Old Testament vow see him as the only one who merits the title, "prince of peace."

It may be a truism but it is still a fact which needs proclaiming, that we do not have peace sectionally or nationally or internationally because we do not have peace within our own individual hearts.

Peace does not come because of the calmness of outer conditions. It comes because of the composure of inner commitment. Even standing in the shadow of Calvary, our Lord could say to his disciples: "My peace I give unto you" (John 14:27). And after the crucifixion, as he prepared to send them out to be both proclaimers and persecuted, he said, "Peace be unto you" (John 20:21).

What did he mean? Well, to be sure, I think he meant the end of conflict and turmoil within the life of each follower. H. G. Wells uses the descriptive phrase "a civil war inside." No more of that! But the reason there would be this absence of discord was because of the presence of dedication. Peace within is possible because of a Person within—Jesus Christ!

One of our most distinguished ministers defines holiness as "inner health." I think it is also a fair definition of peace. Again, this cure, this calm, this certainty, is attained through him.

Alistair MacLean tells of a lovely occurrence that illustrates so well, I think, the point we are attempting to make.

Some young boys were visiting an old seaman who now was home from his travels. As they sat together in his cottage looking out over the sea, the scene was one of almost perfect tranquility. The waters were quiet. The seagulls flew noiselessly. The world seemed hushed. Yet the boys noticed that the greatest serenity of all seemed to dwell in the soul of the old sailor. One of the lads asked, "As you watch, Sailor John, why is there peace and strange gladness in your eyes?" Standing to his feet and stretching out his hands to the west their elderly friend answered, "Because I love one and he is always in my heart." [1]

IV

"And he will destroy . . . the veil that is spread over all nations. He will swallow up death in victory." (Isa. 25:7-8.) Here is the final validation: He is *the Lord of eternity*.

Look once again at these first three affirmations. No longer do we need fear loneliness of soul; he is the presence of God. No more should we be under subjection of sin; he is the Saviour of men. Let there be an end to hostility of heart; he is the prince of peace.

Now look at this last great promise. Death will be displaced. "He will swallow up death in victory," as the King James Version records it. He is the Lord of eternity.

What triumph this should bring to our lives! We may know his fellowship now. We may be saved through his grace now and be privileged to witness to this precious gift. Likewise peace is ours to know now and to share. Then one day when we have the "summit attained," to quote Browning, we shall find that death but brings us into his nearer and dearer presence.

[1] Alistair MacLean, *Radiant Certainty* (Naperville, Ill.: Alec R. Allenson), p. 134.

He does not simply hold our hand as far as the cemetery. He does not redeem us merely to die. His indwelling peace goes not just to the grave. Paul says we are "a colony of heaven" (Phil. 3:20 Moffatt). And Jesus said, "Because I live, ye shall live also" (John 14:19).

Let us live then in the glad assurance that this pledge, too, has already been fulfilled in him.

A little lad stood outside a department store window looking at the pretty toys. The teddy bear especially held him fascinated. A passing pedestrian heard him say, "I sure wish there wasn't no glass between."

The man viewed the poorly clad boy. Then impulsively he grabbed his hand and said, "Come with me, Son, and you shall have some of those playthings."

The small boy became quite excited and said, "Let me tell my mama," and he hurriedly darted across the street. He did not see an approaching car. The automobile hit him and a few minutes later he was taken to the hospital. However, he was not critically injured.

Later that same day, his new friend brought many an armful of toys to his room. Hugging the teddy bear close to his chest, the little chap cried with delight, "All these toys are mine and there ain't no glass between."

"Now we see through a glass, darkly; but then face to face." (I Cor. 13:12.) The Bible says there is a definite place called heaven. But it begins now when the risen Lord enters our lives, for Jesus said to know him is life eternal.

THAT RADIANT PLEA

*Welcome one another, then, as Christ
has welcomed yourselves, for the glory of
God. (Rom. 15:7 Moffatt.)*

The letter of Paul the apostle to the Christians at Rome
is one of the most important writings in all the literature
of the church. There are three reasons why this assertion is
made.

First, the letter is of great import because of the writer
that composed it. Not only would the early church have not
had its greatest leader had Paul been missing from the
scene, but a great part of the New Testament would be
gone from our Bibles. In the second place, this letter holds
a strategic place because of its contents. Nowhere in the
New Testament is the theology of Christendom so clearly
defined or highly exacted as it is here. In the last place, this
letter is significant because of the congregation to whom it
was addressed. Paul was writing this letter to a rather
strange mixture of Christian folk in the capital of the world.
The church in Rome was composed of two groups: converted Jews and converted Pagans.

How very pertinent, then, is this text—the apostle's ap-
peal to welcome one another.

How very urgent today that our church with all its differences and disagreements hear and respond to this radiant plea: "Welcome one another as Christ has welcomed yourselves, for the glory of God."

I

What does the word "welcome" mean? "Welcome one another, then, as Christ has welcomed yourselves." In order for us to understand this word we must observe that the "then" in the text takes us back to the brief prayer the apostle has just prayed prior to this request.

"Now the God of patience and consolation grant you to be likeminded one toward another according to Christ Jesus: that ye may with one mind . . . glorify God." (Rom. 15:5-6.) We are to forget our differences, our selfishness. We are to represent Christ by being so brotherly, so harmonious that all our actions toward others will be dedicated to the strengthening of a loving fellowship. And this united for God's glory.

Phillips has it: "Open your hearts to one another." We have no greater obligation to the world than this. We have no truer identification to Christ than this. This is what our Lord constantly proclaimed with his teachings.

Here is a man lying in the ditch. He has been beaten half to death. Most likely he is a Jew. A priest comes by but after seeing the wounded man passes by on the opposite side. A bit later, the servant of a priest walks that same road, sees the same man, responds in the same way. But a

Samaritan (and "the Jews have no dealings with the Samaritans" [John 4:9]) came that way and opened his heart to the man in need.

This is what our Lord revealed with his life. The scribes and Pharisees accused him of eating and drinking with tax gatherers and sinners. Even as he died in agony on a cross, he opened his heart to a brigand and welcomed him into paradise.

Look at our world with its clashing economic systems. Look at our nation with its racial tension. Look at our church so often seeking to save itself. If the religion of an open heart will not redeem there is no hope.

Paul looked at the Corinthian church split by division, marred by immorality, hampered by secularism, at odds over the expression of worship, and gave this marvelous counsel: "Open your hearts wide to me" (II Cor. 6:13 Moffatt). The answer to a weary world and a warring society and a weakened church and a wayward life is a widened heart.

I am thinking of a little seamstress who had the lovely avocation of caring for homeless children. She opened her home especially to little folk who had known a father's care and a mother's love. But due perhaps to an accident or disaster a child had been left without parents, and it was to these she gave the fullest measure of her affection.

One morning word came that a little five-year-old girl was the only survivor of a tragic wreck. The seamstress at once prepared for the coming of the child into the home.

However, one of the older children protested: "We're sleeping three in a bed now. There's not room enough." I have never forgotten her answer. "Dear," she replied, "when there is room enough in the heart, there is always room enough."

II

How may we welcome one another?

There are very few signs of welcome more conducive to encouraging good will than a *glow on your face*. I tell the people that compose our congregation a smile instead of a scowl will mean more in welcoming strangers than any sermon the minister preaches and any anthem the choir sings.

Aristotle was right when he said the face is the mirror of the soul. If God lives within, then the glad reflection without is going to give assurance to others. Luke says that when the Jews "saw the boldness of Peter and John . . . they took knowledge of them, that they had been with Jesus" (Acts 4:13).

There is a certain layman who today is an earnest Christian. He was won for Christ by a man who never said a word to him. The man simply had a radiance about him regardless of climate or circumstance. His friend sought the reason behind such joyful certainty, and he, too, came to know the source.

Stanley Jones is right in his admonition to us that if our

hearts rejoice in Christ, we should by all means notify our faces.

Not only may you be a welcomer by the glow on your face but also by the *grip of your hand*. A disciple from Cyprus named Joseph gave this kind of witness. His fellow disciples nicknamed him Barnabas because of the lift, the encouragement, he always gave. When the young church at Jerusalem was suspicious of Paul, we read that Barnabas took him by the hand (Acts 9:27 Phillips). When young Mark still had not won the respect of his brethren because of his cowardice, again we read a similar phrase: "Barnabas took him."

A man in the West gave this as his reason for experiencing the coming of Christ in his life: "It was the pressure of a friend's hand in mine." Don't sell this short. There is a lot of gospel in it.

Then you may welcome folks by the *kindness in your voice*. The temple police were sent out by the chief priests and Pharisees to arrest Jesus. They returned empty-handed. When questioned as to the reason, they replied, "Never man spake like this man" (John 7:46). Of course, our Lord was frank, but there was an unspeakable tenderness in his tone and the officers found it irresistible.

A layman whom I know stands in front of his church on Sunday and welcomes guests. One person told me that sometimes her greatest blessing received on Sunday morning was to hear the kindly greeting of "Happy" Walker. And there are people all across that city who will testify to the same experience.

Now all these factors we have mentioned occur because of one central particular: the *love in your heart*.

This makes the glow and the grip and the kindness possible. This is the spring from which the living water flows. "By this shall all men know that ye are my disciples," said our Lord, "if ye have love" (John 13:35).

Now God needs you and he needs me to welcome the sinful and suffering and sorrowing into his fellowship. He needs us to receive gladly the ones outside the redemptive brotherhood and make them feel at home. There is just one requirement in order to be used. There is just one element essential for such service. Training will not do it. Etiquette will not do it. Ability will not do it. They will help. But it is the person who has allowed God's love to fill his life who offers the only hope for a welcome men will not reject.

"Why did you join that church?" one Negro asked another who had recently become part of a group whose membership was mostly white. "Because," he answered, "when I entered the sanctuary seeking Christ, a white usher held out his hand and said, 'My brother, you are welcome here.'"

III

Why should we welcome one another? Paul makes this radiant plea because in Christ's mercy and love he first had been welcomed himself. "Welcome one another as Christ has welcomed yourselves, for the glory of God." He is literally saying because you have found joyous access into the presence of the Master, so you are to be the glad way of approach to his presence for others.

Then the apostle adds this meaningful phrase: "For the glory of God." It would seem, therefore, that as we extend open hearts to our fellowmen we are reflecting the very person of God. With arms outstretched to encompass all men we are saying by this action, "This is the way to the Father."

Paul is but reminding us here of the way in which our Lord came with his open arms and open heart inviting us to experience the kingdom. Jesus was forever extending winsome invitations to men to receive his love and to know his grace and to share his truth.

It is interesting to note that his ministry opened and closed with such appeals. When Jesus first began preaching, two disciples of John the Baptist were strongly attracted to him. "Where dwellest thou?" they asked. "Come and see," he answered (John 1:38-39). It was, as a friend of mine has suggested, an invitation to discovery.

Then in the shadow of the cross, we hear him say, "Come, ye blessed of my Father, inherit the kingdom prepared for you" (Matt. 25:34).

There is this difference between the two invitations. The first was given to men to come into his fellowship and to

71

know more about him. The second was given as a result of what the disciples, to whom he was speaking, had done for others.

This invitation is appropriate as we compare the plea Paul makes in our text. The apostle is requesting that we do something for others. The Master makes our worthiness to enter heaven hinge on what we have done for others and only invites us to share his eternal glory on the basis of what we have been willing to do for those in need.

"As Christ has welcomed yourselves," said Paul. And was not the Master continually welcoming, opening his heart, doing for others? There was a blind man who needed sight. There was a multitude who needed bread. There was a harlot who needed purity. There was a robber who needed forgiveness.

They are out there across our land today. Some are ill. Some are lonely. Some are lost. Some are in their youthful tender years and need the guidance of one who knows the way. Who will welcome these for God's glory?

There was once a layman in a small country chapel that had compassion for a young lad who was not a Christian. Time after time he sought out the boy and explained to him the life abundant. At length he had the distinct joy of introducing the youth to Jesus Christ.

How that deacon must have rejoiced in heaven that God used him to help the lad discover he had a heart filled with music. Listen to his song:

But all thro' the mountains, thunder-riven,
And up from the rocky steep,
There arose a glad cry to the gate of heaven,
"Rejoice! I have found my sheep!" [1]

And how Ira Sankey must have rejoiced all his life that a man loved him enough to welcome him as he himself had been welcomed into the arms of the Redeemer.

This is our greatest obligation. But more—it is our highest privilege.

[1] Elizabeth C. Clephane, "The Ninety and Nine."

BUILDING CHRIST'S CHURCH

*Thou art Peter, and upon this rock I will
build my church. (Matt. 16:18.)*

"I will build my church." This is the task Jesus is
seeking to accomplish through those of us who follow him.

Immediately prior to our Lord's pronouncement of his
mission, Peter had openly declared that Jesus was the
Christ. This, it appeared, was the requirement that had to
be realized before one could be yoked with the Master in
the sacred employment of extending the kingdom.

"Upon this confidence in me," Jesus seems to say, "upon
this certainty about me, this commitment to me, I dare
build my church."

Now it is not our intention at this point to presume
upon the Lord's program for building. But on observing
certain conditions in our fellowship both at home and
abroad there appear obvious needs that must be met.

Through Christ it is our high privilege to help build a
church that can redeem the world. What kind of church
can accomplish this task?

I

We must be a church that *lives*. Jesus not only loved life
but he loved to talk about it and did so often. "I am the way,

the truth, and the *life,*" he said (John 14:6). "I am come," he proclaimed, "that they might have *life,* and that they might have it more abundantly" (John 10:10). And again, in discussing with a lawyer love for God and man, he said, "This do, and thou shalt *live*" (Luke 10:28).

One pointed at Phillips Brooks and said, "There goes the livingest man I ever saw."

The Pharisees were not seeking to compliment Jesus as he himself suggested concerning a statement in Luke's gospel. I like Dr. Phillips' version of the intended insult. "The Son of Man came, enjoying life, and you say, 'Look, a drunkard and a glutton, a bosom friend of the tax collector and the outsider!' " (Luke 7:34.) He was the livingest man their world had ever seen.

This life that is radiant and lifting and victorious Christ wants his church to know and to share.

Years ago I came to know a family that I loved and appreciated. Heartbreak often guides us to truth that happiness could never show. The young husband in that home lay in the hospital for seven years, a living dead man. Since he was paralyzed both mentally and physically, oxygen and intravenous feeding were all that gave him existence. I visited that room during the day and again at night. Always I would find his devoted wife or faithful mother, or both of them together, lingering by his bed. They seemed to say by their loyalty, "Perhaps one day this one we love will be restored to life."

To me it is a picture of the eternal God standing watch

over many of his children. So great was his love that he gave his only Son that whosoever believeth in him should have everlasting life. There is a report, C. S. Lewis suggests, that one day we are going to come alive.

Oh! that this were the advent hour. The living Christ— the living church—this is all that can restore the lifeless and redeem the world.

II

We must be a church that *loves*. First and foremost is this love for God.

After the resurrection, when Jesus met Simon Peter by the sea of Galilee and examined his credentials for dynamic apostleship, he felt one question was all inclusive. "Do you love me?" he asked. Not "do you love sheep," nor "do you love to tend sheep?" Love for the flock and love for their feeding depends upon our love for him.

This is what led that gallant band of itinerant laymen across the Roman Empire. So deeply did they cherish their Master, so fully were they yielded to his cause, so completely were they imbued with his presence that persecution, pain, and death were faced and borne through the strength of love's glory.

Love for our brothers is the direct consequence of our love for God.

Our Lord did not say, "In this particular the world will recognize you as my agents, if you regularly attend the synagogue." And going to church is important. Neither did he say, "Because of this example humanity will realize you are my associates, if you are faithful in your giving." And we should share our possessions. Jesus never said, "This is the practice by which your contemporaries will observe that you are my followers, if you are seen performing acts of benevolence." And this a Christian will do. But Jesus said, "By this shall all men know that ye are my disciples, if ye have love one to another" (John 13:35).

Do not simply declare as a witness that God is love. That is true but in personal testifying it may sound a bit cold. Say to men, "God loves you."

When I come home after an especially difficult day, I strongly suspect it would encourage my spirit very little for my wife to meet me at the door and say, "Marriage is love." But when she takes my hand and says, "I love you," the thermometer of my heart begins to rise. Let us say it then to all men, "God loves you." And what is more expedient, let us live it in their presence.

I am thinking of a church that so beautifully translated their love for God into love for folks that their fellowship became known throughout an entire area. They helped the needy. They waited upon the ill. They ministered to the fallen. They brought hope to the lonely.

One night, a man seeking aid came into the city where the church was located. Hailing a policeman, he asked, "Can you tell me the place where they heal broken hearts?" Now explain it how you will, the officer escorted the man to that particular church.

If one came to your city or to mine with a need that only a friend of Christ's could answer, would he be directed to our church because of the love we constantly reveal?

III

We must be a church that *lifts*. There are three definite things that each of us may do in order to make the lifting power of the church possible and available for all men.

First, we may pray. How essential Paul felt this to be. Not only did he solicit the petitions of the saints. He asked eagerly for the prayers of the struggling young churches.

What an exponent of prayer was our Lord. Listen to his words to Peter: "Simon, behold, Satan hath desired to have you . . . but I have prayed for thee" (Luke 22:31-32). That is what changed the reed into the rock. This is how a fickle follower became a powerful proclaimer.

I do not see how any church can be serious concerning the mission of Christ in the world if it is not devoting itself to prayer.

There are numbers of the people in our local fellowship who hold up their minister to the throne of grace in daily intercession. There are some who have definitely indicated that this is part of their Christian obligation. I am sure there are many others who share this ministry although they have never said so openly.

Just recently I was impressed rather suddenly to visit a certain home. As I stopped my car in front of the house, the person I was attempting to see rushed out from the

porch. "Thank God, you are here," was the opening saluta-
tion; "I am in desperate need of help." We talked and
prayed together and God quieted the storm. But I felt as
I left that someone had been praying, perhaps even at that
very hour, for the Spirit to give guidance.

Second, we may give. Now and then I read a book at
our church that is most illuminating. It both cheers me and
distresses me. It is called "The Treasurer's Record." I note
as I scan its pages where one gives much more than he is
able because those causes dear to the heart of our Lord
must not go unheeded or unsupported. Then I observe another's contribution and as I see how lightly he considers his
stewardship when Christ has given all, it fills me with
gloom thinking of the joy he is missing.

Some will disagree with me, but I am convinced that
the more difficult it is to give, the greater is the joy in giving.

A young minister sat watching the crowd putting money
in the offering plates. He seemed little interested in the fact
that the wealthy people were dropping in large sums. But
when a poor woman passed and put a penny in the treasury
he was profoundly stirred. In fact, he all but broke up the
meeting he was so eager to relay the news to his congregation. "This poor widow hath cast more in, than all they
which have cast into the treasury," he said, "for all they did
cast in of their abundance; but she of her want did cast in
all that she had" (Mark 12:43-44).

If God cannot build his kingdom with dollars of dedication, he will do it with pennies of poverty freely offered.

Finally, we may witness. Perhaps it sounds elementary to say this in a sermon, but testifying to people about Christ is the obligation of every Christian. Read again the book of Acts and you will be persuaded that the Holy Spirit did not simply speak to and work through the professional hierarchy of the church. Every disciple of Christ was a sharer of good news; every follower was a teller.

Walk with Philip to Gaza, stand with Peter in Joppa, listen to Paul in Jerusalem, journey with Barnabas to Antioch. They are men filled with the Spirit and thrilled with the privilege of proclaiming it.

Make no mistake about it—there is absolutely nothing so attractive as a man aflame with the gospel of Christ. "If you are on fire," Bishop Denney used to say, "people will come to watch you burn."

The redeemed fellowship has many responsibilities. The poor need bread. The illiterate need teaching. The lonely need companionship. The aged need attending. The ill need care. But our greatest interest must be the lost who need salvation. And the person concerned must be as that already mentioned—one with a glowing heart.

"Why do you wish to return to China," one asked a missionary who had come back home broken in health. "Because," he answered, "I cannot sleep at night for thinking of them."

This is the kind of commitment Christ must have from his church if the kingdom of God is to come.

DRAWN TO THE CROSS

*I, if I be lifted up from the earth, will
draw all men unto me. (John 12:32.)*

I have a friend who is unusually close to me. When I
stood outside the Jerusalem wall beside Golgotha's summit,
I wished that he could have been there to share the experience with me. Amid many thoughts one recurring reflection was of our friendship.

"Ralph," I said, when we were together again, "as I
stood at Calvary, I thought of you." "Wallace," he answered,
"that means a great deal to me. But the thing that means
more to me than all else is that one stood there two thousand
years before you did and thought of me."

Here at Calvary is where God's thought became incarnate. It is where God's love became most evident.

"I, if I be lifted up from the earth, will draw all men unto
me." Observe the magnetism of Calvary—how we are attracted to the Cross.

I

The Cross claims our attention.

There is a haunting verse in Matthew's account of the
passion story. The mock trial is over. Along the way of

sorrow our Lord has shouldered his heavy burden. When the hill of Golgotha at last is reached, he is nailed to the weight he carried. Then we read, "And sitting down they watched him there" (Matt. 27:36).

Through the centuries millions have joined the soldiers in taking a lingering look at the Cross. Certainly this view of the crucified Christ has not always redeemed. But it does open the door to conversion. We do know that the Roman commander "glorified God" the day he witnessed the entire scene at Calvary. (Luke 23:47.) And we have it on record that another of the soldiers extended to our Lord his last earthly ministry by giving him a drink. (Matt. 27: 48.) It is the considered conviction of the Christian church that a man cannot be devoted to the Lord's service unless he is first drawn to the Lord's sacrifice. Yes! and claims it as his own dedication. Did not Jesus say, "Whosoever will come after me, let him deny himself, and take up his cross, and follow me" (Mark 8:34)?

When the mob of frenzied insurrectionists stormed the palace in Versailles during the French Revolution, suddenly they came to a chapel. There they saw a painting. It was Christ on the Cross. The mob became quiet. The crowd was hushed. Not until that painting was removed did the holocaust continue.

We must, as his disciples, not allow the vision of Calvary to become blurred. We must not allow the Cross to be unseen or unspoken in our witnessing, preaching, teaching, living!

Drawn to the Cross

Luke says that when the time was come for the Master to give his life, "he steadfastly set his face to go to Jerusalem." Really, all through his ministry he was looking in the direction of Calvary. And so must we. A minister friend of mine has evening altar services at his church. He noticed that though his little boy was but five years old, he began going along with the others to the altar when the lights were lowered and the organ played. "Mark," his father asked one night as they were returning home, "what do you say to God at the altar when you go?" "Daddy," he replied, "sometimes I don't say anything—I just look at the cross."

The Cross must be our goal before it is our glory; it must have our attention before it has our allegiance.

II

The Cross commands our respect.

Whatever else may be the emotion, few men can gaze at the suffering Redeemer without having a sense of high regard. In many instances high consideration leads to deep consecration.

> See, from his head, his hands, his feet,
> Sorrow and love flow mingled down;
> Did e'er such love and sorrow meet,
> Or thorns compose so rich a crown? [1]

I find that I am often speaking to people seemingly un-

[1] Isaac Watts, "When I Survey the Wondrous Cross."

concerned; many indifferent to the claims of Christ and his church. Sometimes I encourage them to draw near to Golgotha in their imagination. I ask them to see this "sorrow and love flow mingled down." I have known men, moved in no other way, to see life in a totally different perspective when they evaluated Calvary. And, too, when they realized their unworthiness in the light of such sacrifice.

A few days ago I received a letter and here is a paragraph that illustrates so clearly and meaningfully what I am seeking to say. I have not altered it.

Recently I had a thyroidectomy. I was in St. Thomas Hospital and, of course, on the wall opposite my bed where I saw it every time I raised my eyes was a crucifix. I was extremely nervous and upset with toxic goiter and all I could think of the night before surgery was the crucifix. Because of my physical condition they did not dare give me a general anesthetic and I was forced to go through the operation under local. There was so much infection that the novocaine did little more than deaden the outer layer of skin and it was almost like having no anesthetic. Just before I mercifully lost consciousness from pain, as plainly as though it were really there, I saw the crucifix and my last thought was, "Christ, how you must have suffered and it was for people like me."

I dare say that it was this experience of redemptive respect that led her to becoming one of the most loyal laborers in our church. Yes, and one of the choice souls I have known in a lifetime.

III

The Cross changes our will.

"I, if I be lifted up . . . will draw all men," said Jesus. Of course, we may refuse to be drawn. "Jesus did not come to make salvation certain," Claude Thompson reminds us, "he came to make it possible." It is ours to receive. It is ours to reject. He stands knocking. He does not come forcing.

But when we give Calvary our genuine attention and when we stand before the Cross with sincere consideration, then it is that the Redeemer, through this act of redemption, speaks to our hearts and transfigures our lives. For, you see, a man cannot be "ego-centered" in the shadow of his sacrifice. He cannot continue seeing all life in the range of self-interest when he views One who has given all.

> And from my stricken heart with tears
> Two wonders I confess:
> The wonders of redeeming love
> And my unworthiness.[2]

Never have I known it to be better said than the way a South African expressed it when this wonder transformed him. "It should have been me," he insisted, "it should have been me." Or, consider these words from the man of Tarsus who likewise knew the joy of self-releasing and Saviour-receiving: "I am crucified with Christ: nevertheless I live; yet not I, but Christ liveth in me: and the life which I now

[2] Elizabeth C. Clephane, "Beneath the Cross of Jesus."

live in the flesh I live by the faith of the Son of God, who loved me, and gave himself for me" (Gal. 2:20).

Listen to a layman: "It suddenly occurred to me as I looked at a crucifix that I put him there. I am going to spend the rest of my life telling how he forgave me for doing it."

Listen to one of the twentieth-century's greatest preachers whose vision of Calvary completely altered his life and ministry and who afterward saw all the world as a crucifix: "I see the cross set up in every slum, in every filthy over-crowded quarter, in every vulgar flaring street that speaks of luxury and waste of life. I see Him spring up at me from the pages of the newspaper that tells of a tortured, bewildered world." [3]

IV

The Cross controls our witness.

We first look at Calvary with real earnestness. When we do, a kind of sublime awe engulfs us. Then we are transformed by divine love. We then seek to reveal this redemption—to share this salvation with others.

Now the Cross coupled with the empty tomb formed the main line of the gospel message advocated by those who belonged to the daring young church. They gloried in the realization that they could endure it. "They [the apostles]

[3] As quoted in *You Can Preach* by G. Ray Jordan (Westwood, N. J.: Fleming H. Revell Company, 1951), p. 31.

departed from the presence of the council, rejoicing that they were counted worthy to suffer." (Acts 5:41.)

They gloried, too, not only in the realization that they could endure the Cross but in the fact that they could exalt the Cross. Listen to Paul's words to the Corinthians: "For the preaching of the cross is to them that perish foolishness; but unto us which are saved it is the power of God" (I Cor. 1:18).

So today! It must be the glory of our gospel—the heart of our herald.

Some years ago I was invited to preach at a youth rally near St. Louis. On the way, I stopped by to see a friend that I deeply loved and greatly trusted. I do not always agree with his theology but I have complete confidence in his commitment. "I am going to preach about the Cross," I told him. "What shall I tell them?" "Tell them," he said with deep conviction, "that when we begin with God, we begin at Calvary."

That's it! Here is where our witness must start—and continue.

"I, if I be lifted up from the earth, will draw all men unto me." It was true then. It is true now. It will be true forever.

The Scots of Bruce were wavering. Suddenly one of the officers on a white charger took the heart of Bruce in a chest and holding it high in the air cried out, "Oh, heart of Bruce, lead on." His soldiers then could not be restrained. The Christian Army, too, has a call to arms.

When Morning Comes

> Onward Christian soldiers,
> Marching as to war,
> With the cross of Jesus
> Going on before.

May this be God's hour in our world, in our witness. "Oh, cross of Christ, lead on!"

WHEN MORNING COMES

When the Sabbath was over, just as the first day of the week was dawning . . . an angel of the Lord came down from Heaven, and rolled back the stone. (Matt. 28:1-2 Phillips.)

The phrase, "as day was dawning," means more than the coming of light to the earth. It means the coming of light to the soul.

The black night of crucifixion and all its counterparts—pain, disbelief, separation—was over. The morning of new faith, new hope, new joy, above all, new life had arrived.

There is a symbolic statement in the Gospel of John. The scene is in the Upper Room and Jesus has just reported that one of his own will betray him. When John asked which one he meant, he replied that it was the one to whom he would give the bread. He then proceeded to hand it to Judas and we read, "So Judas went out immediately after taking the bread. And it was night" (John 13:30 Moffatt). Of course, it was night in the city of Jerusalem, but it was night in the heart of Iscariot.

And in a very real sense it was night in the hearts of all the disciples—both on the eve of Calvary, during those dreadful hours when our Lord was on the Cross, and then after the torture had ended.

But now the dawn appeared. The day had come. The light dispelled the gloom. Christ had risen!

Now what did the coming of morning mean to those who had been so filled with shadows? Let us look at four followers and be aware of the fact that what happened in their experience happened in the lives of many of his followers, and can happen now!

I

For Peter the coming of Easter morning meant a broader world. The Gospel of Peter had been a gospel for Jews only. But a risen Christ opened the door to the far horizons. Listen to the Master's words: "Go and teach all nations" (Matt. 28:19), and again, "Ye shall be witnesses . . . unto the uttermost part of the earth" (Acts 1:8).

It was a great day in the life of the big fisherman when he was able to say, "Of a truth I perceive that God is no respecter of persons: But in every nation he that feareth him, and worketh righteousness, is accepted with him."

Is this truth not desperately needed in our world, our nation, our church today? "Love the Communist?" we ask. "Impossible!" No! Their conversion is impossible without receiving this love. Yes, and our consecration is impossible without sharing it.

That question, "Love the Russian?" is not new. "Love the Assyrian?" cried Jonah. "Love the Greek?" cried Peter. Only when morning comes to the heart, only when the day dawns in the soul, only when the resurrected Lord lives in your life, can the whole world be your parish and every man be your brother.

As we have suggested, this is the answer to the world's need. It is the answer to our nation's need. Martin Luther King was recently addressing a group from one of our large southern universities. After he spoke, a discussion group meeting followed. There were many good serious questions raised. However, after a bit, one young critic asked, "Is not intermarriage your inevitable goal?" "My friend," Dr. King answered, "we do not want to be your brothers-in-law. We want to be your brothers."

So! if this is the remedy for the world's need and our nation's need, it is the answer to the need of the church. If God is our Father, then as his children we are all brothers. Listen again to our Master, "There shall be one fold and one shepherd."

The church of the risen Redeemer must not be simply a religious institution. It must be a redemptive fellowship. The church is not a building. It is a brotherhood. The church is not a sanctuary and property. It is the Saviour and people working together in harmonious concern under God's guidance in quest of any and all who need hands to lift and hearts to love.

I don't remember where I heard this story but there is a lot of gospel in it. Two newspaper boys were standing on a corner in a certain city. Near them was a man, or perhaps I should say a half-man. His legs had been cut off above the knees. He was selling pencils. A car pulled up to the curb and a man got out. Walking up to the man with the pencils, he said, "My brother! I have looked for you—to care for you. What I have is yours." Then he picked him up in his arms and carried him to the car and off they drove. "Wouldn't you love to have a brother like that?" asked one lad. "Yeah," answered the other, "but wouldn't you love to be a brother like that?"

I must confess this is the thing that causes me constant alarm. I am not so much distressed that our church people may go to hell in some distant tomorrow. But I do see many that are in a hell of the here and now—the hell of indifference and uselessness and seclusion. What worse hell could there be than a church seeking to save itself, then remembering too late God's children who cried for bread?

II

For Mary the coming of Easter morning meant a bigger faith. How sad she was that day when she mistook him for the gardener. I doubt seriously if even the inner circle—Peter, James, and John—loved our Lord more than Magdala's harlot who became Easter's herald. In great grief she spoke to him: "If thou have borne him hence," she said, "tell me where thou hast laid him" (John 20:15-16). The Master replied with but one word, "Mary." She knew there was only One who could speak her name like that. She remembered when first he had spoken her name and the Mary of the darkness had become the Mary of the dawn.

She would not doubt again. Witnessing took the place of weeping. Instead of tears shed there would be testimonies shared. From the tomb mourning she would go to the disciples rejoicing. Here were her glad tidings: "I have seen the Lord!" (John 20:18 Phillips.)

But, you ask, could Jesus have changed so much in a few days? Why did she fail to recognize him? Well, of course, death and the extreme agony of Calvary had doubtless made a difference in his appearance. Then, too, his dress was not the same. But here is the main reason she did not know him—she was searching for a dead man! And this is the reason that today many do not have an awareness of the reality of his presence. We look for a Jewish rabbi, an itinerant teacher, a crucified martyr.

To be sure, we do not say it in terms like these. We are more academic. We say, "I believe in the Jesus of history." That is why so many remain outside the tomb without joy or peace or certainty.

But when we look for a resurrected Savior, a risen Lord, an everlasting King, we find him on this side of Good Friday, not as the Jesus of history but as the Christ of eternity.

III

For Thomas the coming of Easter morning meant a believing mind. You remember Thomas was not with the other disciples when Jesus appeared to them that first Easter Day. When they informed him that they had seen Jesus risen and alive he simply did not accept it. "Except I shall see in his hands the print of the nails, and put my finger into the print of the nails, and thrust my hand into his side, I will not believe." (John 20:25.) What Thomas actually meant was this—he doubted completely their testimony and he had absolutely no confidence either in the receiver or the revealer.

But eight days later Jesus came and stood in their presence. "Peace be unto you," he said, and turning to Thomas he invited him to do what he had claimed he had to do in order to make his faith valid. Thomas, however, did not need to feel the marks caused by spear and nail. A greater sense than touch had taken possession of his life. His faith became real, not because of what his hands felt but because of what his heart knew.

Then our Lord said, "Because thou hast seen me, thou hast believed: blessed are they that have not seen, and yet have believed" (John 20:29). Either way, you see, is valid. There is so much evidence of his reality that seeing can be believing.

> There is so much of God about:
>   I hear his voice when children shout,
> I see his smile when the sun is bright,
>   and feel his presence in the night.
> His beauty shows in feathered wings;
>   I see His hand in many things.
> There is no room for strife and doubt
> When there's so much of God about.[1]

[1] Ruth K. Kent, in *War Cry*.

But Jesus was also suggesting that believing can be see-ing. Do you recall the demon-possessed boy the disciples were unable to heal? Looking to Jesus, the anxious father said, "If you can do anything, do help us, do have pity on us." Jesus immediately answered the father by insisting it was his faith that would open the door to his son's cure. "If you can," said the father. "If you can!" replied Jesus. "Anything can be done for one who believes." (Mark 9: 22-23 Moffatt.) Then the man declared his faith and Jesus healed his son!

For Thomas this was an experience where certainty led to faith. But I think the Master's purpose for appearing in this instance was so that from this hour on his faith would lead to certainty.

IV

For Cleopas the coming of Easter morning meant a burn-ing heart. Do you remember how Cleopas and his com-panion walked from Jerusalem to Emmaus with weary feet and broken hearts?

Jesus had been crucified. The exciting, wonderful dream of a coming kingdom had ended. "We trusted that it had been he which should have redeemed Israel," they said (Luke 24:21). But that trust was in the past tense.

As they walked together discussing the promises that seemed to have perished, suddenly a young man drew near and began to walk with them. They told him about their leader who had come and they spoke of his words and deeds. But his attempt to bring all men into a fellowship of love had ended at Calvary.

Then the stranger began to speak. He did what all good ministers should do. He interpreted the scriptures. What a sermon that must have been! The living Word revealing to them the written word. Reflecting upon those moments later in the evening, Cleopas would say, "Did not our heart burn within us, while he talked with us by the way, and while he opened to us the scriptures?" (Luke 24:32.)

Then with this glad glow of assurance, they returned that same hour to Jerusalem to share the reality of his resurrection. The radiance they revealed we, too, have the privilege of presenting. Only a burning heart can help Christ save a sinning world.

"Are you a Christian?" a consecrated layman asked a woman in a hotel lobby. After they had exchanged a few preliminary remarks, he presented to her the tidings of great joy. Just as he left, the lady's husband joined her. "What did that man want?" he questioned. "He asked me if I were a Christian," she answered. "That is a very personal question," said her husband. "Why didn't you tell him it was none of his business?" "Oh," she replied, "if you had looked at his face, you would have thought it was his business. Indeed," she continued, "you would have thought it was his only business."

This is the chief business of the sons and daughters of the King! Because he rose, it is our happy privilege to tell all the world the morning is here!

AFTER PENTECOST

When the day of Pentecost was fully come, they were all with one accord in one place. (Acts 2:1.)

And they continued steadfastly. (Acts 2:42.)

I believe it was my friend Jim Calhoun who first told me the story of that indomitable little American tourist in London.

This small elderly lady seemed rather unimpressed even in the Gothic magnificence of Westminster Abbey. She listened and looked with only mild interest as the one who was conducting pointed out the burial places of England's great. Even the spot where the monarchs are crowned brought little enthusiastic response.

As the tour of the great church was concluding, however, she suddenly came to full and fervent life. "Young man," she said to the bewildered guide, "You haven't told us the most important thing. Is anybody getting saved?"

The "most important thing" about Pentecost was not a sound like that of a rushing wind. Nor was it the tongues which were like flames of fire. Here is Pentecost's supreme significance: somebody got saved.

I am really not certain that the disciples themselves were saved in the New Testament sense of this word until this particular experience. Salvation means we are saved from something and for something. These men who had been so concerned with their own affairs now gave themselves with wreckless abandon to Christ for the sake of others.

Their primary question, too, came to be, "Is anybody getting saved?" as they sought through the strength of the Spirit to answer that query with a glad affirmative.

Now what happened as a result of Pentecost that made it possible for men to be saved?

I

First, there was *prayer in the home*. Of course, there would be prayer henceforth in the church, but actually the fellowship was meeting at this time in the home. We must note, too, that if prayer was a result of Pentecost, it was also a cause of Pentecost. Concerning the disciples, prior to the indwelling of the Spirit, we read, "These all continued with one accord in prayer" (Acts 1:14).

The disciples realized how weak they had been before Christ had come in his risen power. Do you recall their inability to heal the epileptic boy? After the Master had cured the lad, they asked Jesus why they had not been able to accomplish this task. The Lord replied that this particular ministry required prayer. (Mark 9:29.)

They knew now they could not continue in their own strength. So after Pentecost "they continued steadfastly . . .

in prayers" (Acts 2:42). And what did this prayer effect? Here is what Luke says:

"He [Stephen] full of the holy Spirit." (Acts 7:55 Moffatt.)
"He [Barnabas] full of the holy Spirit." (Acts 11:24 Moffatt.)
"Peter, filled with the holy Spirit." (Acts 4:8 Moffatt.)

So! In his grace and in his strength and in his presence they found victory for themselves.

But since Pentecost had brought concern for others this eventuated in prayer interest. They were not selfish in their praying. They interceded constantly for others. Take one example for instance.

Peter had been chained in prison in Jerusalem. But Luke says, "Prayer was made without ceasing of the church unto God for him" (Acts 12:5). (During this particular incident Christ's followers were gathered at Mary's home in earnest intercession for Simon.) Then what happened? "Behold, the angel of the Lord came . . . saying, Arise up quickly. And his chains fell off." (Acts 12:7.)

This can happen today! Some chained by mental and physical illnesses can be set free. The chains of sin can be broken. Men chained by indifference can be released. "All things, whatsoever ye shall ask in prayer, believing," said the Master, "ye shall receive" (Matt. 21:22).

II

A second result of Pentecost was that there was *purity in the heart.*

After Peter had finished preaching on that memorable day, the crowd was under a deep sense of conviction. "What shall we do?" they asked. "Repent," was Peter's first response (Acts 2:37-38).

When one is confronted with the living Lord, he always feels his soul's inadequacy. There was probably no man in Jerusalem more devout than Isaiah but when, in the temple, he met the King, hear his response: "Woe is me! for I am undone" (Isa. 6:5). Peter's cardinal virtue was not humility, but Luke relates how, in the course of one of their earliest encounters, Simon fell at the Master's feet, crying, "Depart from me; for I am a sinful man, O Lord" (Luke 5:8).

The Holy Presence can never come into a man's heart when it is filled with things he is not willing to give up. Repenting is the first condition for receiving.

Is there anything in your life to which you are clinging, something you cherish more than the eagerness to be filled with new life in the Spirit? You may consider it a little thing, but if it is a hindrance to his indwelling, it must be removed.

I was preaching a few weeks ago in one of our Southern cities and a woman lingered after the altar service to make what I considered an unusual confession. "The reason that I came forward tonight," she confessed, "was to give my driveway to the Lord." Then she went on to explain. "Our driveway becomes an alley when it meets the connecting cutoff to our garage. Late at night young people often drive through that thoroughfare blowing their horns and screeching their tires. My husband works the evening shift, and this noise occurs just as he prepares to retire. I am afraid," she continued, "I make it a habit of losing my religion every midnight. But now along with my temper, I have given this driveway to Christ." Then, with a sheepish grin, she said, "I suppose this is a little thing."

"What does it matter," her pastor answered, "whether it is little or big, as long as it keeps you from the joy of full surrender." Then he added this word that I think came from one of the early church fathers, and I will never forget it. "Really," he said, "it makes little difference whether it is a chain or a thread as long as it holds you from God."

Jesus said, "Blessed are the pure in heart." Did he not mean blessed are those whose hearts are *emptied* of every shadow whether it be a totally dark one or a threateningly gray one? Did he not mean also blessed are those whose hearts have been *filled* with the light, the radiant glow of himself?

III

A third effect of Pentecost was that the disciples had *power in their witness.*

It is rather amazing how many times you find this word "power" in the New Testament after Pentecost. What is the power of the Spirit? Well, certainly this question would draw a number of answers from many quarters. My answer, I suppose, is very elementary indeed. But I think the power of the Spirit is caring for people with Christ's kind of concern. I think it is feeling for all men with Christ's kind of love. I think it is serving the world's needy with Christ's kind of affection. And this, too, is a gift from God.

Before Pentecost the disciples had been fearful. When Jesus was arrested they left by every available exit like frightened children. When Jesus was crucified they were not, as some have suggested, frustrated and bewildered men. They were utterly defeated men.

But then the resurrection—Christ with them! And afterward Pentecost—Christ in them! Observe them now. They are not frightened followers. They are courageous crusaders. They are not defeated disciples. They are masterful messengers.

Across the Roman Empire they go with this witness of power, this victorious love. They are certain it can redeem the world, for they know it has redeemed them.

It is pertinent to note that these witnesses for the most part were uneducated as far as formal education was concerned. Peter and John are referred to as "unlearned and ignorant men" (Acts 4:13).

But they were men who had yielded themselves completely to Christ, and evangelism is, in the first place, not an aptitude that is grown but a heart that is given.

To be sure, the pulpit needs this witness of power. But 90 percent of the church is composed of the witness from the pew that must not fail in its courageous testifying.

You would have to think a long time before you could

declare that England has had a greater preacher than Spurgeon. And a layman introduced him to the Master. You would have to consider diligently before you could say that America has produced a stronger evangelist than Moody. And a layman won him for the kingdom. This, then, is power: Christ shared from a concerned heart.

IV

The last point we shall consider is that after Pentecost there was *preaching in the world.*

There is an old story that relates how Francis of Assisi invited one of his disciples to accompany him on a preaching mission. The lesson is eternally relevant. Francis found three people in the city that day who had differing needs, and by simple acts of love he was able to answer their wants. Just as the great saint's duties that day revealed preaching as not only an exhortation of the lips but a proclamation of the life, so is this necessary in our day.

More and more I am noticing how few people who have not committed their lives to Christ even concern themselves by attending church at all. Of course, there are many who have made professions of their faith that are not living up to them. Therefore, we must be the church scattered, the body of Christ extended to any and all areas of need.

Mark says that after the risen Saviour had made his identity known to his followers that "they went forth and preached every where" (Mark 16:20). That is, with both the words of their mouths and the witness of their lives, they sought to bring people to a saving knowledge of Jesus Christ. Some took the gospel where it had not been received. Some stayed to cultivate what was done by faith's pioneers. Some helped by caring for the widows and orphans (Acts 6:1; James 1:27).

It made little difference to these devoted servants whether the world placed prestige on their actions. Peter led three thousand to Christ at Jerusalem; Philip led one man to the Lord in the desert. They were not interested in distinction but dedication. To redeem men was their first thought; renown from men, their last. They were not seeking the commendation but the consecration of the world.

I have been remarkably impressed by the redemptive activities David Wilkerson is instigating in the slums of New York. He has written a book called *The Cross and the Switchblade* in which he tells something of his labors with the teenage groups in that city.

I once heard him tell how he won a young dope addict and drunk for Christ. The youth became one of his most faithful and loving proclaimers. One night, his former cronies cornered him and because he would not renounce Christ, the gang knifed him nearly to death. When Wilkerson reached the hospital, the lad managed to gasp in pain, "I bear on my body the marks of the Lord Jesus."

When we proclaim Christ like that, then our sermons and ourselves will give evidence that the Spirit has come—that Pentecost is here. Then it is that the kingdoms of this world will become the kingdoms of our Lord.

THE YEARNING CHRIST

I stand knocking at the door. If anyone
listens to my voice and opens the door, I will
come into his house and dine with him, and
he with me. (Rev. 3:20 Phillips.)

Here is the sublime picture of the ages. This portrait is
what religion is all about. It is what the Bible is all about.
It is what life at its best is all about. Christ stands before a
closed door seeking admission.

Now this scene is at once a picture that inspires both
pathos and praise, grief and glory. Does it not touch us with
a bit of sadness to see the Prince of Heaven standing at a
door, even as a beggar might come pleading, humbly be-
seeching those inside to open? But does it not touch us at
the same time with an unspeakable gladness that he actually
wants to companion with us and break bread at our table?

The church at Laodicea is a good example of the church
today or, for that matter, of our own individual lives. Of
course, the people that lived there were not hostile to God.
Neither are most of us. Neither were they ablaze with the
spirit of complete allegiance. And how many Christians today have "hearts afire" as did Cleopas and his companion
on the Emmaus Road?

No! the problem is actually very much the same. The

church then was neither red-hot nor ice-cold. It was luke-warm. The people who compose our church now are for the most part respectable, decent, kindly folk whose hearts are neither fiery nor frozen, and it is at our door that the Master comes knocking.

Let us look at this scene under three definite headings.

I

First, there is *the action God takes.* Jesus said, "The Son of man is come to seek and to save that which was lost" (Luke 19:10). It is the same as the picture in Revelation. Luke says he is seeking. John says he is knocking.

It is urgent that we catch the tenor of this first point. It is not simply the paramount point of a sermon. It is the inaugural point of the gospel. The initiative God takes. The offer he makes. The invitation he gives.

Man has the chance to open the door because the Lord stands before it and knocks.

There is a sentence in John's Gospel, taken out of context, that illustrates this truth so pointedly. A dear friend of Jesus, Lazarus, had died. Our Lord purposely delayed his trip to Bethany. Lazarus' illness was intended to bring glory to God, Jesus said. This was the time he had chosen to teach a memorable lesson. He wanted his followers to know that the resurrection was not an event but an experience. It was not a date on the calendar; it was his presence in the heart. This he taught Martha with words. It was something he would teach Mary with a deed. (The raising of Lazarus.)

Therefore, after she had been instructed by Jesus, Martha went in quest of her sister Mary, saying, "The Master is come, and calleth for thee" (John 11:28).

That is the good news of the written word. Jesus has entered the scene. Or to use Paul's words, "When the fulness of the time was come, God sent forth his son . . . to redeem" (Gal. 4:4-5).

It is the good news of the Living Word, for the gospel is more than his coming to the world. It is his calling that extends to all men. There is little doubt about his coming: his birth in Bethlehem, his ministry through Galilee, his death at Jerusalem. But "I am come that they might have life, and that they might have it more abundantly." (John 10:10.) So! he is the Jesus of history, but he is also the Christ of experience. And his mission and message is one of endless action and constant activity in the quest for man's salvation. He seeks. He saves. He calls. He dies. He rises. He knocks.

I remember years ago knocking twice at a man's door that I was seeking to introduce to Jesus. My first visit proved futile for the man had not yet returned home from work. We were having a service at the church that evening and I told his wife I would try to come back again before the worship hour. The second time I knocked, he was at home. The invitation to accept Christ was extended and my friend became an earnest Christian. Not long afterward, he said, "Mr. Chappell, you will never know how deeply I appreciate your knocking at my door that second time." I replied, "Mr. Lee, it was my joy to return the second time, but there was One that had knocked at your door a thousand times and it was he that led me to knock and you to answer."

To what lengths has the Galilean visitor gone, what numerous attempts he has made to enter the lives of us all! "I stand knocking at the door."

II

In the second place, there is *the response man gives.*

A lad of five heard his minister read the words of this text. "If anyone opens the door," he read from the pulpit, "I will come into his house." The little chap could not get the words out of his mind. That night before going to sleep, he said to his father, "Daddy, I wonder if the people opened the door. Do you know? Did they let him in?"

Have you? Have I?

Well, there are some who are not even aware that the Divine Guest has come calling. There are a thousand and one other things that occupy their time. "Your servant was busy here and there," said one of the characters in the Old Covenant, and he has many an offspring when it comes to our sacred responsibilities. Busy here and there while a Saviour's unchanging love and unfailing love becomes unwanted love. Busy here and there while the great promises of God go unheeded. Busy here and there while the great invitations to the soul go unanswered. Busy here and there while the world races toward hell and so many who could be a part of the cure remain a part of the malady.

O my soul! when will our power-mad world and our selfish-crazed society be still enough to listen as the King of Glory with nail-scarred hands uses those hands to knock at the entrance of our lives?

There are yet others who know that he is seeking admission into their hearts, but they are not ready to offer what one has referred to as "hospitality to the highest." They crack the door perhaps but do not open wide. The Divine Visitor, however, will not force his way in. He depends upon our willingness to open fully. That is the reason why so many in the New Testament slip as Judas did into the night. They were not willing to give Christ the right of way to a complete entrance. So the rich young ruler kept his wealth, Demas kept his greed, and Felix kept his harlot. And Jesus still pleads for our surrender to be complete. We often look at what we have. Perhaps we gaze a bit wistfully at what we miss, but still keep the door closed.

But there are those who open the door gladly and fully and even give him the key to the house.

Listen to William Borden, that young Galahad of Golgotha: "Lord Jesus, I take hands off, as far as my life is concerned. I put Thee on the throne in my heart." That is what it means to open the door.

I like the story I heard recently of a small chap who was standing with his father gazing up at Holman Hunt's famous painting. This painting is, of course, the twentieth verse of the third chapter of Revelation placed on canvas.

After they had stood looking at it a few moments, the father said, "Son, some day you must open the door." "But daddy," his little laddie responded, "I have never closed it." Perhaps that is why the Lord Jesus said, "Whosoever shall not receive the kingdom of God as a little child shall in no wise enter therein" (Luke 18:17). It is the children and those with child-like hearts that keep the door constantly open.

III

Then there is *the companionship we share.* "I will come into his house and dine with him, and he with me." This is the climax of the gospel. He has knocked. I have opened.

If a man is known by the company he keeps then the friends of Jesus certainly reveal much about our Lord. Take a look at the beginning and ending of his life. Humble shepherds welcomed his birth. Despised criminals shared his death. It was a fact that all during his ministry he seems to have been a faithful companion of the outcasts and degenerates. Even the disciple upon whose confession he proposed to build his church was a swearing fisherman. His enemies criticized him for eating with sinners, and his disciples marveled that he would speak with a prostitute.

I know of nothing that Jesus ever said which offers our world more hope than this: "I am not come to call the righteous, but sinners" (Matt. 9:13). Paul reminds us that "all have sinned, and come short of the glory of God" (Rom. 3:23). I think most sinners fall into two groups.

There is first the sinner who fails to give his life to Christ. Here is one of the saddest statements our Lord ever made: "Ye will not come to me, that ye might have life." He stands knocking but we refuse to allow him entrance even though he is the only one whose presence brings both meaning and music to our lives.

It occurs to me that God does not primarily desire possessions. He wants persons. His supreme interest is not in your substance. It is in your self.

Gypsy Smith was once playing with his little girl, Zillah, when a friend approached to chat with him. The famous preacher gave his daughter some money, thinking this would satisfy her, and turned to engage his acquaintance in conversation. But Zillah was not content with the coins. She cried out, "Daddy, I don't want your money. I want you." And that is what God wants.

If the good shepherd, about whom Jesus spoke, could not be satisfied until that last lost lamb was safe in the fold, what about the Divine Shepherd? How through the ages his great heart longs for each lingering lamb and each straying sheep.

Do you recall how Jeremiah heard God commission him with what really became his lifetime task: "Run ye to and fro through the streets of Jerusalem, and see . . . if ye can find a man" (Jer. 5:1).

The eternal God across the centuries is on a manhunt. Have you allowed him to find you? Then, there is the sinner who fails to live his life with Christ.

When we think of the church's greatest day of blessedness, we usually think of Pentecost. But so often we miss the purpose of this joy. It was not so much a blessing to receive as it was a blessing to release. The real joy of Pentecost was the desire to share this gift of the Spirit with all men. "Ours is not to grasp the Spirit," Ray Jordan used to tell his students, "but to channel the Spirit."

That is our task. I really am not sure that we have any other. One who knew the joy of the Christ-life said, "The length of time God permits us to stay here is not related to a certain amount of work he wants us to do so much as to a certain closeness of relationship to himself he wants us to attain." And the closer we draw to him, the more compassion we shall know. Surrender first and service next.

Not long ago I knelt at the altar with a college lad who had not put everything in his life at God's disposal. There was no pretense. He desired the gladness of complete allegiance. "How can I know this joy?" he asked. "Ronnie," I answered, "God loves you. Christ gave his life for you. The Holy Spirit is at this moment seeking admission into your life." So he opened the door and admitted the Divine Presence into his heart and now in a distant city he proclaims this priceless privilege to others.

Our Lord will dwell *in* you but he will also speak *through* you. Even now he yearns to have your heart as his home, your life revealing his love. At your heart's entrance he knocks. Through this open gate he will beckon others. Will you let him in?